WINK

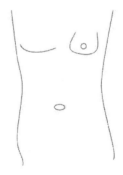

2

Prologue

This is the story of my relationship with breast cancer. Hundreds of thousands of women are diagnosed with breast cancer every year. My hope is to share some insight into feelings that can accompany this disease that impacts our feminine existence and thus inspire others to share their story.

I did not include an in-depth portrayal of all the people who helped me through the illness. I didn't talk of the hugs, the cards, the prayers, the blessings, the meals, the phone calls, etc. that made this journey possible. Because of all the love I felt, from so many people in so many ways, I was strong enough to write. This is my way of honoring all the people who supported me in my journey.

I am grateful to everyone in my life, especially my family. I appreciate all the extra loads of laundry and additional chores my husband, children and mom did on my behalf. I am even thankful for the everyday arguments that occurred. They conveyed to me that everyone knew I was bigger than the disease.

For those who have gone through a similar experience, I hope you find a way to tell your story; for those who are just about to embark on the journey, though I am sorry you have to go through it take notes. You will emerge a stronger person for it.

To all women: Get mammograms, do self breast checks and never let anything defeat you.

With admiration and gratitude,

Dawn

WINK

Chapter One

To me, age is irrelevant but there are certain things one must do to keep the body in working order throughout the span of a lifetime. Luckily, I have people in my life who remind me of what those things are. One particular requirement of aging is getting mammograms. Generally speaking, recommendations have been for a typical woman with no-risk or family history, to begin somewhere between the age of 35 and 40. The insurance companies are trying to modify these medical guidelines, but for me the changes did not occur in time to alleviate the guilt that had been building in my conscience. So, after a year of putting it off (and that doesn't mean I am 36), the shame had risen to a level that sufficiently haunted me - it was time to bite the bullet and schedule the appointment. (Actually, I couldn't face my mother-in-law returning from yet another trip and having her ask me, yet again, if I had scheduled my mammogram only to offer my sheepish grin and reply, once more, "Not yet.")

By trait I am a self sufficient person and a penny pincher. I don't busy myself with too much primping, (though I have vowed to my husband not to cut my own hair any more), too much fashion (though I have assured my teenage daughter that I won't show up to her school functions in clothes more than one decade old), and if something needs doing I usually figure out how to do it. Until I met my husband, who has a completely different outlook, I even changed the oil in my car. I don't go out of my way to seek the help of others and I certainly don't look for problems, which makes preventative health care a bit less compelling for me.

The good thing is that with everything becoming a one-stop shopping place, medical care included, I knew the mammography clinic was very convenient to get to. It was located in the hospital where my gynecologist was. I finally telephoned the office and booked the appointment. With the accomplishment of, among other things, 'baseline mammogram' written in my calendar - in pen - the day was a success.

Having committed to the date I pondered the experience I would soon be partaking in. I hadn't been avoiding the encounter due to all the horror stories one hears of squished bosoms. Although the descriptions of chest wall fat being compressed between two adjustable paddles, turning this way and that can make the hair rise on the back of some people's necks quite frankly, after two natural childbirths I couldn't imagine that any medical procedure that took less than fifteen minutes could be tortuous. For me, in addition to the shear avoidance of what I perceived to be optional encounters the evasion was more personal. The idea of standing with a cloth cape and revealing one breast then the other ranked up there with the discomfort of exposing oneself for a pap smear. Though there was little mystery as to why I was abstaining from such treachery, it was only a matter of time before I would be grateful for the awkward exam. Having followed through with the mammogram I managed to dodge a bullet that may have one day had a more catastrophic out come.

I went in for the baseline mammogram, had my four pictures taken and went merrily on my way. It was rather uneventful and surely nothing that would leave a lasting impression. At most I figured the results would be sent to my gynecologist and in a year or, (more realistically) two, when I saw her again, she would praise me for being a responsible person having taken care of my female requirements.

WINK

Chapter Two

My expectations were dashed by a phone call from the mammography clinic requesting that I return for additional pictures. Though the desire to see me again was unexpected, I really didn't need the reassurance that the gal on the phone was offering. I had worked in a mammography clinic in my 20s and knew it was very normal to be called back for additional views on a baseline mammogram. It made sense to me to have a clear depiction of what my breast tissue consisted of so in years to come the comparisons could be accurate. I didn't think much of it, unless of course you count the perpetual thoughts about the inconvenience of returning to the hospital. But, still determined to reply something other than "Not yet" when my mother-in-law returned from her trip I dutifully followed through with the appointment.

My husband and mom had each asked if they should accompany me to the appointment for moral support but I think the look on my face, implying that they were crazy, proved a verbal response unnecessary. *"I'm going back for films - big deal,"* I thought. I brought a book to read and decided I'd enjoy the unexpected time of leisure. I was reading about geographical bliss, a book where the author was in search of the happiest place on earth, which turns out to be a little ironic. I certainly wasn't at the happiest place on earth. After progressing through the changing rooms and locking non-valuable items in a cabinet I joined the other women who sat in the waiting room. Attempts had obviously been made to create a comfortable atmosphere with cushioned couches, tropical fish tanks, and a big screened television displaying a benign show, but the bottom line was we were all dressed in unflattering capes, clutching our purses with bungee cord keys to our lockers dangling from our wrists waiting to be summoned to a game of Russian roulette.

When my name was called I gathered my belongings and quickly answered "Here" as if respectfully responding to a classroom roll call. I was led into a room with a large x-ray machine and a little computer. The routine was pretty much the same as the first time except that, rather than just taking the four medial lateral and lateral pictures the photo session went on and on. Realizing I was going to have to become a little less modest I tried to focus my thoughts on the technician. She was friendly enough and provided clear commentary on each image she took. If someone had been all worked up about being 'recalled' the information would probably have been comforting.

In hind-sight, I guess I should have realized that things weren't panning out to be as "routine" as I had thought. Maybe I should have picked up on a sense of pity that the technician felt every time she stepped back behind the Plexiglas wall to examine the quality of the picture that was displayed on her computer screen or the extra compassion she expressed as each x-ray revealed a sadder truth. She must have realized the devastating news I was about to receive and yet could say nothing. Perhaps I should have been more perceptive and detected the lack of normalcy in the numerous extra pictures that were taken but instead I obediently complied with all the positioning and posing, believing it was all relatively common.

Finally I was told I could get dressed and return to the waiting area. Then the technician informed me that the doctor wanted to discuss my films with me. (OOPS, maybe my husband and mom had been on to something.) Fully clothed, I was taken to a quiet little room to wait for the radiologist. Looking around the space I now occupied, I saw a couch, a chair and a little table with a box of Kleenex on it - I wasn't getting the best vibes.

The radiologist joined me in the room and told me that there were some suspicious areas on the films and I would need to have a biopsy to determine what they were. Without warning, tears began to trickle down my face. She quickly reassured me that 80% of all biopsies were negative. After conveying a bit more information she left and was replaced by a nurse who was ready to tell me when and where I needed to be for this "usually negative" biopsy. Having regained control of what I have often referred to as my "leaky faucets" my demeanor returned to business as usual. I left with a brochure in hand and a date for the biopsy feeling a little slighted that none of this had been "normal." My baseline mammogram had escorted me down an unexpected path.

WINK

Chapter Three

Once in the car I called my husband. This was a perfect reminder of just how different time and space are for each of us. He answered, sounding as though he had me on speaker phone, laughter in his voice and company in the back ground. He is lighthearted and witty and this time was no different as he joked about something that I can't even now recall. I have never wanted to hang up the phone so badly. I couldn't get a word out, stunned by the gap between his mood and mine. He immediately sensed something wasn't right. I managed to ask him, through a steady flow of tears, if he could call me when he had a minute. Of course, true to character, he was immediately available for me right then and there and anxiously awaited the reason I was upset. "I have to have a biopsy" I sobbed. I felt a little embarrassed for the discomfort I must have caused in his office by the sudden interruption, but embarrassment gave way to a sense of calm from the love my husband expressed.

"Everything is going to be okay," he reassured me. I agreed and admitted I didn't really even know why I was crying. Not one to dwell on things, I didn't accept the notion that anything was wrong with me. I think my weeping came more from the fact that things hadn't gone as I had planned. He talked more, and I listened, agreeing that we would get through this and it would be no big deal. He asked if I would like him to come home and I assured him I was fine and there was no need for that. We ended our conversation with our usual, "I love yous". The routine seemed to help me return to a calmer state of mind.

Rather than going straight home I decided to stop by a local department store; I yearned for some normalcy. I roamed the aisles, gathering routine items, pretending it was a run-of-the-mill day. When I was finished with what had turned into walking aimlessly through the store, I paid for my things, got back in my car and continued toward home oblivious to my surroundings.

When I arrived home I was greeted with the friendly hello I had become accustomed to receiving. My mom had been staying with us for a while since she was at a time in her life where she had the freedom to enjoy leisurely travel and spending oodles of time with her grandchildren who adored her.

Upon seeing my face my mom flashed me an uneasy smile. It must have been mother's intuition, or maybe the remnants of tear stained eyes, but her first response was that she should have gone to my appointment with me. I reassured her I was fine and that there had been no need for anyone to have come. I did admit that I hadn't anticipated the outcome of the appointment so well, and then broke the news that

I was going to have to have a biopsy. She comforted me with her motherly love, not allowing her shock and disbelief to show through. I knew she was sad knowing that her baby had a battle ahead, but we were both so grateful she was with me and would be able to help us through this unforeseen situation.

When my husband, Mike, got home from work we discussed the notion of telling our children. We decided to tell our 14 year old daughter, Karli, but to hold off on telling our 10 year old son, Marcus. Though we didn't want to burden her, Karli is too inquisitive and perceptive not to notice when things are awry. She becomes curious and probes for information. If not reassured with the perimeters of the truth she tends to imagine the extremes. Knowing the particulars always seems to set her mind at ease and typically, in these types of situations, she rises to the occasion with amazingly deep understanding.

With a lighthearted start we conveyed exactly what the doctor had told us. We explained that I was going to have a precautionary biopsy of some calcifications that showed up on my x-rays but, according to the doctor, the pathology usually came back negative. She felt honored that we trusted her with the information and, after discussing a few relevant questions we all carried on with our everyday lives.

WINK

Chapter Four

A week later I returned to the clinic for my biopsy, this time with Mike by my side. I checked in with the receptionist, then we took a seat in the lobby. As I looked around I wondered who was there for a routine mammogram and who would be leaving with a scar such as the one I was about to receive. I determined those with partners where probably in the same predicament as I and was certain one gal who sat, already in her cape aside her husband with tears streaming down her cheeks was surely going to have some type of biopsy.

It had been determined that since my suspicious findings could not be felt (or palpated as they like to say in the medical field) the protocol was to do a stereotactic biopsy. This is a procedure where the radiologist uses a specialized machine, which generates images to guide the biopsy needle to the exact area where tissue samples are extracted. It sounded very precise, which is good considering the microscopic cells they were hoping to collect.

After disappearing to dress in the familiar cape, I was led through various doorways where I rejoined Mike. Together we ventured into the room where I would have the procedure done. After a bit of chit chat with the nurse and the radiologist I was positioned, face down, on a metal table with a hole for my breast to hang freely - that is, until the technician placed it in a permanent hold with a mammographic vice. Needless to say I was beginning to evolve from my normal modest disposition.

The procedure went as scheduled, obtaining "perfect" tissue samplings. Humor accompanied me with my husband in attendance. I was not spared the tasteless jokes that seem to come to our minds during stressful times. A true sign of his comforting, though not for the faint of heart, he teased of how I was trying to outshine him with the threat of cancer, one upping his diagnosis of multiple sclerosis five years prior. Though an onlooker may find our crude sense of humor appalling, it's always at our own expense and had gotten us through nearly nineteen years of marriage.

Once I was bandaged up, given a cooling pack for the surgical site and a red rose as an apology from the nurse we were free to leave. Though advised to go home and rest we stayed true to our nonchalant style and decided we could relax better with some entertainment. Our afternoon came to an end with a visit to a local movie theater for a matinee of *Star Trek*. I packed along extra ice packs to ensure a comfortable ride into the galaxy.

Unbeknownst to everyone, the entire weekend I impatiently waited for the results. Every time the phone rang I was sure it was going to be someone calling to tell me that this whole adventure was over. Occasionally I thought about "what ifs?" but those ideas were quickly laid to rest with my readily available mental checklist: I am a healthy, somewhat fit, not really overweight (unless you look at the weight stated on my driver's license) relatively young lady with zero family history of breast cancer.

Finally Monday afternoon, alone at home, I received a phone call with the results: "Pathology indicates DCIS, Ductal Carcinoma In-situ" the voice dictated. After a lengthy explanation from the radiologist I ignorantly asked, "So, my family is going to want to know, do I have cancer? What should my response be?" The radiologist confirmed the not-so-normal predicament I seemed to be in. "Yes, you do have cancer, but it is very treatable and most important, curable." She ended the conversation by apologizing for having to give me such undesirable news and informed me of numerous appointments that had been scheduled on my behalf, starting the next morning at 7:00 a.m.

The line went dead and I thought to myself, not, *Oh my gosh, I have cancer!* but rather, *Are you kidding me? I hate appointments!!!! My freedom is gone!* I hung up the phone and found myself looking over the jumbled notes scribbled across a piece of scratch paper. Just like that, my life had changed forever.

First I called my husband. "I'm coming home," he told me without leaving me any time to convince him otherwise; I guess it was a bit of a shocker. When he arrived home, he comforted me with a tender, reassuring hug as tears fell down my cheeks. The reality had begun to sink in but the gentleness that he held me with, no words spoken, seemed to simply say, "Everything is going to be all right."

WINK

Chapter Five

I can't quite remember who we told next my mom, my sister, my dad, my in-laws, my brother-in-law at this point it was just immediate family. We decided not to tell Marcus yet because we still felt we lacked enough information to know what all this really meant. We decided to wait until we had some more concrete details to share with him, along with a plan for moving forward. This was very true to our family characteristic, since a common question that lingered in our home was, "So, what's the plan?"

The next morning I was dutiful and arrived early for my MRI. I changed into a karate looking outfit then was escorted into the imaging room. Discreetly, the technician slid my top off and positioned me, lying face down, into yet another contraption that cradled my breasts. Who knew there were so many pieces of machinery geared towards breast imaging? On the table, face down, I slid into a circular hole in the machine. Following directions to keep very still, I attempted to drown out the constant machine gun sounds of the MRI machine by focusing on the melodic voice of Nora Jones coming in through my headphones. To prevent claustrophobic feelings, my apparatus had a mirror that reflected a beautiful poster of nature for me to look at. After the first round of images were finished I was excavated from the machine and received an injection of contrast; a dye that differentiates between tissue types; in my case - cancerous and non-cancerous tissue. When the second series of imaging was complete the table slowly returned to its starting position and I was free to leave. All and all, it was pretty uneventful.

With my medical appointments piling up, my mom was able to get the kids to the places they needed so there was no disruption in their schedules. As information trickled in we continued to keep Karli in the loop. She seemed to manage the ambiguity of the information well and felt privileged that we shared this knowledge with her.

To conclude my anthology of appointments, all of which had been deemed necessary in order to gather data regarding my cancer diagnosis, I had a meeting scheduled with a surgeon. Originally I had tried to change the date, because it fell on Karli's 15th birthday, but evidently many people relied on this particular surgeon's expertise. I couldn't get another appointment for three months so I opted to keep it as planned.

After filling out another 'new patient' packet my husband and I were escorted into the examination room. We sat in silence, perusing the various certificates of medical achievements that hung on the wall. I don't know if it was the coincidence of our daughter's birthday, but it didn't feel much different than the times we had waited, side by side for my gynecologist to appear for our pregnancy exams.

Shortly, a quiet knock sounded and the door opened revealing a gal who looked a bit younger than I, in a white doctor coat, a skirt and heels. She had a petite build, which was in line with the rumors I had heard of her being a marathon runner, and a natural look of beauty. She extended a friendly introduction, with a darling south-western accent all, conveying a warm and comforting feeling. Mike and I were able to communicate our approval to each other as the surgeon proceeded to discuss my case. She had pathology reports for us, MRI pictures on display for our viewing and a plan of action. We liked the fact that she was cutting (excuse the pun) to the chase.

Our suspicions were confirmed by the discussion and data. Though the cancer cells themselves were contained to the ductal system and non-aggressive, it was the amount of space they consumed that left no other options: the course of treatment would be a left breast mastectomy. She showed us the images on the computer screen. Looking at them, even our non-medical eyes could recognize the difference between the left and right breast tissue. One side appeared to be gray, like what you would expect to see on an x-ray and the other side looked ghostly with white swirls branching every which way. This didn't affect my demeanor until the conversation changed from a factual exchange of information to a more personal one. The mere question of the ages of our children brought me to tears. I eventually managed to choke out that it was our daughter's fifteenth birthday and we had a 10 year old son. On that note, we made our way out to the scheduling desk. My original plan to wait until the end of summer break got shot down however; I felt some sense of control as I deferred surgery for two weeks rather than taking the suggested appointment the following week.

Once the mastectomy was scheduled, as a token of sympathy the nurse handed me a bag filled with items from a variety of cancer groups. Walking past the receptionist's desk with pink raccoon eyes and departing gifts in hand, I received the icing on the cake, puppy dog eyes with a turned down lip. I know those looks! Those are the looks I try to hide when I go to my dad's chemo appointments and see women my age hooked up to IVs. Am I one of those people now? Someone everyone feels sorry for? I couldn't get into the elevator fast enough to escape the pity and reality of my circumstances.

WINK

Chapter Six

Thinking about the statics I had just become part of I realized that personally, I knew of only one person who had previously had breast cancer. Though I hadn't known her at the time of her struggles, it had saddened me years ago when I had heard of what she had gone through. Now, as the diagnosis became more real, it was she who came to mind.

I struggled with wanting to talk with her about her experience and wanting it all to go away. I didn't want to pry into something so personal and bring up painful memories from her past, yet I was scared and lonely with this diagnosis I knew nothing about. I yearned for the comfort of someone who knew what I was going through.   Finally, brave enough to accept the predicament I was in, I reached out to her for guidance and she welcomed me with open arms. She comforted me with both sadness for what I had to go through and faith that I would conquer it. She reassured me that I had not offended her by my discussion of breast cancer and she conveyed that women who have experienced breast cancer become open books. She was ready and willing to help me in any way she could.   I was immediately comforted by her valiant survivor attitude.   She inspired me to move forward with courage and to obtain as much information as possible.

With her advice, paralleled with the requests of my in-laws and countless others, Mike and I decided to seek a second opinion. It was a bit awkward, seems as how we liked all the doctors we had already encountered.   We had never been ones to spend afternoons looking at numerous houses when on the homeowners trek or to test drive countless automobiles when seeking a new car. Typically we knew what we liked right from the start. We were completely content with my medical panel but, if there was a chance that something had been misinterpreted then this was the time for scrutiny.

For my medical corroboration we chose a much respected doctor who had specialized in the breast field since its infancy. We arrived in his office on a Friday afternoon, just before a holiday weekend. As directed I brought copies of all of my medical records, including a CD with numerous digital MRI and x-ray images of my upper torso. I filled out the standard new patient packet and then Mike and I were led to a very sterile room; it had an examination table that looked to be evenly spaced between all four walls and two sitting chairs. Left alone, behind closed doors, Mike and I each took a seat.

We sat in the room, unattended for an uncomfortable amount of time. We joked that we had been forgotten and would have to spend the long weekend locked in the barren room. Finally the doctor came in and introduced himself. He was obviously more seasoned than the doctors I had already met with which, perhaps, contributed to his abruptness.

Though Mike and I had rehearsed what we wanted to ask we were caught off-guard when the doctor candidly asked, "Why are you here?" Staring blankly at each other I figured I had nothing to lose and answered, "We were hoping that there had been a mistake in the interpretation of my films and that I actually didn't have any form of breast cancer." Then I looked at Mike happy with my response.

The doctor did not entertain my suggestion for even a split second as he confirmed that the data had been correctly interpreted by all of the doctors. He offered that I could get a second opinion from a different pathologist but added that he wouldn't recommend it. He told us that my options were to have another biopsy, to more clearly define the extent of the calcifications but that it would most likely just add another procedure to the inevitable mastectomy. He also offered a nipple sparing mastectomy but even with the limited knowledge I had, Ductal Carcinoma In-situ by definition is contained in the ducts, which of course lead to the nipple so in my non-risk taking opinion nipple sparing was not an option. Mike and I listened to each of the choices, none of which seemed to be viable unless my only desire was to elongate the whole painstaking process.

When all was said and done, Mike and I walked out of the office perplexed by the encounter. Mike couldn't have said it any better when he turned to me and asked, "What the hell was that?" We were both mystified by the lack of clear validation despite no apparent alternatives. We weren't sure if we had offended the doctor by asking him for a second opinion rather than coming to him first but Mike and I left confident that we were in good hands with our previously selected team of doctors and unfortunately, their diagnosis.

Now with a master plan in place Mike and I discussed a strategy for sharing the news with Marcus. The dilemma was that he had a baseball tournament all weekend long and we didn't want the news to mess with his head; we also didn't want to run the risk of him finding out from someone other than us. Karli had gone away for the weekend with some friends, minimizing the chance for random inquisitions, so we decided Sunday after the tournament would be best. Fortunately it was a long weekend, giving him extra time to process the thought of his mom having cancer.

We had read through some of the pamphlets the surgeon's office had given us. Many of them had ideas on how to talk with children about cancer, age-appropriate issues and approaches. This came in handy, as Marcus first thought Mike was joking when he shared the news, a true testament to our sense of humor. I had never so badly wanted to be able to say, "Yes, Daddy is just joking!" followed up with a reprimand of how sick of a joke it was and that it wasn't funny at all. Unfortunately we had to simply say, "No, it's not a joke." We could tell from the look in his eyes, he was devastated! Mike did a fabulous job explaining that it was curable, that I was going to be just fine and I was not going to die from it. I added that although it was sad it was merely a bump in the road. I told Marcus that aside from not being able to play basketball and jump on the trampoline with him for a while after the surgery that it was going to be okay. We told him the plan, and then I left the room so the two of them could have a little man to man time.

When it was all said and done we felt Marcus took the news pretty well. He had a classmate who had just gone through the same thing with her mother, so at least he had a concrete situation to compare everything to and could feel confident that it would honestly be okay.

Throughout the evening Marcus was true to character and shared his various philosophies with me: "Mom, I think God knows you are strong and like challenges," and "Actually, since everything is going to be okay this is a good thing. Now you can know how Daddy feels with MS and he can know what you feel watching him have it. Then you will be okay and things will be back to normal." He was processing the information in a way that made sense to him. It warmed my heart listening to him.

Once the cat was out of the bag Mike felt we needed to tell our friends. Being in the spotlight is not my style, so he managed to spread the word as nonchalantly as possible. I had wanted to send out an email to those he told to reassure them that this was really no big deal and plead not to send flowers or give me painfully sympathetic looks when I saw them but when I actually sat down to write it, it seemed a bit too presumptuous and egotistical. Rather than flowers, I wrote, if someone wanted to send something I would love pebbles, something small, that wouldn't die - that I could do something with when everything was over. Mike thought it was a bit silly, pebbles? As I read through what I had written, it did have a bit of a fable ring to it. Why not breadcrumbs like Hansel and Gretel? And it felt more like I was calling attention to myself than minimizing it. The letter was unsent and flowers began to appear.

Though I was incredibly moved by the gestures, my surroundings began to feel like a funeral home. Colorful petals lined the countertops, but slowly each one would drop, lifeless and dreary, and just as the last flower was about to die a new wave of color would appear in a delivery truck. I dreaded the death that each vase held so I began clipping the flowers before they had a chance to die.

One day I spent the whole afternoon gluing various flowers to paper to make stationary that I could use to write thank you notes. In the end it was the ugliest piece of paper ever concocted, and it too ended up in the garbage. I resorted to drying the flowers, determined to make potpourri when everything was over. I decided I would fill sachets and send them to all my loved ones with a sincere appreciation for the generous support they had shown. After this revelation I was able to look at the flowers with a new sense of gratitude and even more appreciation. I no longer saw death; rather, I saw a multitude of love and care that would carry on in beauty. Perhaps the flowers were a step to understanding everything was not in my control.

WINK

Chapter Seven

Once the diagnosis was confirmed, the plan was in place and loved ones told, I set foot on my alternative healing route. Never having been completely committed to Western medicine, I felt it was a perfect opportunity to investigate the unconventional wisdoms that were available. Certain I had the power to set this cancer mishap all straight, I began my journey.

With Louise L. Hay's book, *Heal Your Body* in hand, I read of the emotional reasons the cancer had taken up residence in my body. It was no surprise to me to find that cancer represented deep hurt and longstanding resentment. As an adult child of our times and having delved into childhood hurts, I was a little disheartened to find that twenty years of therapy had not eroded away any developing cancer cells. Since I was not willing to step aside and relinquish control, I realized that perhaps the work I had done only touched the surface of my psyche. Or maybe the past two years of trudging along to my father's lung cancer appointments had taken a much more poignant toll on me than I had known. Now aware that these demonstrative blocks existed, I expanded my reading to investigate the places the cancer had chosen to reside.

Breast problems indicate not nourishing yourself, overprotection and over-mothering. I have a teenage daughter who would attest to the latter and I would agree 100%. I haven't been able to find the loving balance between holding on and letting go. Perhaps it will be part of this trek. Also, it's true that I find much more joy in doing things for others than for myself, and I am a self-proclaimed over-protector. According to the book's explanation it had really been only a matter of time before breast cancer appeared.

So, to truly piece my situation together (for the avant-garde interpretation), I was envisioning that my overprotective parenting styles, which came from pent-up angst due to unresolved childhood issues, was eating away at me and in order to not pass some dysfunctional hereditary dis-ease on to my children I had better get my shit together and clean up this mess.

This was not really the job a woman that had just been diagnosed with breast cancer wanted but obviously I had a lot to lose if I ignored the facts.

Step two in my unorthodox healing of cancer: I visited an energy healer and explained what had been going on. Though I am not 100% committed to Western medicine, I am not 100% committed to the alternative either - but more so than my husband, who is a 99% skeptic.

With nothing to lose, I was sure that my commitment to getting on the right track would bring about a newfound truth by the time of my surgery on June 10, our nineteenth wedding anniversary. So I left the energy healer's office with a few vitamin supplements, some positive affirmations and the intention to replace my coffee drinking with green tea. I felt good about being in control and bad about the concern this whole silly misunderstanding had generated. I was rejuvenated with the awareness of my body and soul and my ability to have them working in conjunction with one another.

As each day passed I continued to juggle the two medical philosophies. Since I could hardly sit back and explain to my family how I would be fine drinking tea and seeing a shrink, I proceeded to meet a variety of cancer doctors who explained their role in aiding with the cure.

Mike had to go out of town for business so my sister joined me for my appointment with the radiation oncologist. She knew all about the looks I feared, sitting amongst other people in the waiting room, since she had been to all of our dad's appointments too. But we shared a good laugh here and there, despite an occasional tear, and eventually were escorted into the oncologist's office.

To avoid judgment of our father's care I will simply say my sister and I were very grateful for the medical care I was receiving. The doctor, a professional looking, young, African American man wearing a suit and wire framed glasses, first provided us with a brief bio which included that he was a Harvard graduate. He then offered a slew of information and answers to many of our questions. He confirmed that I was in good hands with the surgeon I had chosen, as she had performed surgery on his wife and the results were exceptional. He provided us a deeper understanding of Ductal Carcinoma In-situ and didn't even laugh when he asked me why I thought I had cancer and I responded with my alternative healing psycho jargon of it coming from not being able to set clear boundaries, being overprotective and such. He suggested some more traditional reasons, like my age and the geographic location of where I live (The great Northwest, known for its lack of sun, which can contribute to vitamin D deficiencies and which have been linked to breast cancer). Perhaps these were all said to help minimize any self-defeating judgments but they came across as factual data.

Though originally I had been a bit bewildered as to the reason for my visit with the radiation oncologist, since the chance of having to have radiation treatment was rather slim, I felt fortunate to have met with him. I felt more informed than when I arrived. It was a successful encounter, pleasantly shared with my sister, who seemed crushed I had to go through this whole mess at all.

WINK

Chapter Eight

With surgery on the horizon I began preparing myself for what I wouldn't be able to do post-surgery: end of the school year parties, teacher gifts, shopping for summer camp packing lists - my mind raced and often I felt like I was accomplishing nothing. I would walk into one room to do something only to think of something else I should be taking care of instead.

It was out of character for me to be on a schedule that wasn't my own. I had always enjoyed staying up late, savoring the last days of the school year as I wrapped tokens of appreciation. I had grown accustomed to collecting the children's contributions for mementos for their teachers, all the while reminiscing of the growth each one had made over the year and how they impacted my own children. These traditions were cut short and I was forced to accept the loving help of my friends to finish the room parent duties. News had traveled fast even through the chain of little voices in the fourth grade room, and helping hands were extended from every direction.

One afternoon I received a call. Pleasant as ever, my friend so caringly fumbling over her words, "Is what I hear true?" One can only hope that you are sharing the same thoughts when asked such a question, because I admitted "it" was true. There had only been one "it" I was aware of, but living in a small community one can never know what stories can surface. "I'm so sorry" quickly confirmed that we indeed had both been talking about cancer.

Though many people called to express their concern, which I appreciated from the bottom of my heart, I will forever remember this particular call. It was so courageous, so pure and extended with the innocence of a child. There have been so many times in my life where I have wanted to extend my compassion or sympathy to someone, yet I haven't for fear of intruding on their sorrow. Never had that seemed more appalling than when I was on the receiving end of the empathy. I had such admiration for my friend who acted out of the goodness of her heart to share her concern for me. I had not been offended in the slightest; rather I was honored that she extended herself through the awkwardness of revealing the sad truth. My goal is to remember this act of kindness as I continue my life long journey. It certainly left a lasting impression.

Once the news spread so did the warm wishes. Even friends of friends and friends of family were sending me cards. People were offering to bring meals, take the kids, and give rides or to help in any way possible. I even had offers from friends willing to donate extra fat tissue for the reconstruction of my breast. The generosity seeping from people's hearts filled me with a sense of awe. I felt so unworthy of such kindness - not because of low self-esteem, but mostly because in my mind's eye I was okay and didn't need it. It was as if all this was being wasted on me.

One day I mentioned to Mike that it seemed ridiculous that I felt fine but the doctors said something was wrong with me. He inquired, "Would you rather feel bad and there not be something they can fix?" Without going into detail we both knew that I was the fortunate one. Having had to live with MS for over five years already, I had seen the pain he continued to go through. He even struggles to walk on many occasions. How could I complain about the irrationality of disease and diagnosis? Having experienced less than a month of the nightmare of disease I quickly decided to count my blessings instead of wallow in my misfortune.

My mom continued to help keep normalcy in the house as Mike and I attended various doctor's appointments. She quickly took over many household chores and, even more importantly, games of basketball with Marcus and driving times with Karli. God certainly had a plan when he paved the way for her to reside with us.

I continued with the unconventional remedies of drinking tea, eating greens and saying affirmations - still sure this whole interesting misunderstanding would be over soon. I welcomed the idea that, before too long light would shine on the validity of alternative care and that I might even end up on Oprah, speaking of how my breast cancer was cured. I added grapefruit juice and seed extract to my routine but as surgery grew closer I found myself in a place of limbo. I felt I would betray my family if I were to take additional vitamins. The nurses had advised to stop taking wacky supplements at least two weeks prior to surgery so they wouldn't interfere with the procedure, or in my mind, make me bleed to death on the operating table. However, I felt I was doing an injustice to the complementary care I was receiving by not following the suggestions to a

T. After all, how could I truly believe I would be healed if I wasn't doing what I was told to do? But I had to follow my heart: family first. That is the choice you make when you marry and become a mother. My own desires or rationalities don't always get priority and even this time I was okay with that.

WINK

Chapter Nine

With surgery two weeks out and everyday tasks taken care of, what could be a better time to go to Las Vegas? Actually, it didn't take much for Mike and his buddies to find reasons to visit the lively city. Over the years every time someone got married there was a bachelor party in Vegas. As we all began to age, monumental birthdays were celebrated in Vegas. We renewed our wedding vows on our tenth anniversary in Vegas. Even when our best man was diagnosed with cancer it called for a trip to Vegas, which of course had set the stage for all other disease infested beings in the group, which now included me, to celebrate in Vegas. Actually, the truth was Mike had planned to be in Vegas for work, and coincidently our friends were going for a non-monumental birthday commemoration, so we decided since I was monopolizing our anniversary for the year we could celebrate a week early in Vegas.

It was nice to get out of town and relax by the pool. I read mindless novels and lounged leisurely in bed. In the hotel room Mike and I consummated our marriage of almost nineteen years, which always seemed to be easier on a trip away from home, with-out the fear of interruption. This time, however, as he caressed my breast I couldn't help being overwhelmed with the reality that the end of this pleasure was in sight. What had originally seemed to be a good idea faded into a sad sense of existence for me. With conviction Mike assured me it was merely a body part, the same statement I had been confidently spouting to him and myself since the revelation of its soon-to-be loss. We joked (no surprise) that although I was losing this one, with-in a year I would have two, new and improved breasts; a more than generous, well thought out twentieth anniversary gift for him. But, all laughs and light hearted jokes aside, I was losing a feminine part of me that, for my whole life had helped create who I was as a woman.

Suddenly I was reminiscing about the piece of fat that had always been a part of my chest. I remembered the embarrassment the lack of its size had brought me in sixth grade when a group of boys sitting behind me were unsuccessful in snapping my bra since I still remained bra-less. I recalled being humored in high school, or flattered, when a car drove by on a cold winter night and a passenger shouted out, "Nice chest!" as my boy friend stood next to me, both of us amused. Thinking of its loss I felt gratitude for the nourishment I had provided each of our children in their infancy and sorrow for the reality that, although I was past my interest in childbearing, I could never fulfill that need again. What I had been so callously able to laugh at now brought a slow steady stream of tears down my face. I reflected on the emptiness I was feeling from the thought of becoming less than a woman.

Perhaps Vegas wasn't the best place to go when losing a breast lurked in one's near future. The place of big lights, big money, big drinks, big everything - including breasts. Eventually it seemed as though I was looking at every woman's chest. Real or fake seemed obvious and although it may be every man's dream to have a "rack" to play with, I was horrified that within a year I could be one of those top-heavy eyesores that everyday women find ghastly and men don't take seriously.

Though it was nice to have some time away with my husband, dooms-day began to weigh heavily on my mind. I was ready to return home to my everyday life where there were enough things to keep me busy and I could compartmentalize the surgery into something that was "no big deal".

WINK

Chapter Ten

Just days before my mastectomy surgery, I was fortunate enough to meet with my soon-to-be plastic surgeon. My mastectomy surgeon had recommended him. In asking around I discovered his reputation depicted him as the best at breast reconstruction, but I had been forewarned that he often lacked bedside manners. Seems as how I wasn't looking for a friend, and I did want a good end result, I wasn't scared off by the threat of insult.

Trudging ahead, I had accepted that I was going to be lopsided and a bit alien-like. I did, however, want a plan in place for the end scene, cheese at the end of the maze, so to speak, for post mastectomy time. On the drive to the office I got a little short with my husband discussing my future size. Probably just remnants from our trip; but reality was settling in and there was no way I wanted to be the looky-loo of the neighborhood.

We went into the office and were greeted by a nice lady who, if I had to make a guess, had dabbled a bit with the services provided by the surgeon. When I completed my paper work we were escorted into yet another doctor's office where we awaited the surgeon. I felt a little self-conscious knowing that the person who was about to walk through the door specialized in fixing things that not only were the outcome of a travesty but also things that could simply be improved upon. Hiding behind my paper cape I still felt naked.

Fortunately I didn't have much time to feel unsure of myself because the doctor came through the door in a thrust. A relatively tall, fit, well kempt man in his 50s sporting a shirt and tie, he radiated a level of confidence which teetered on arrogance. He spoke in very straight forward terms with us which left no room for ambiguity. Though the topic wasn't as pretty as discussing how he could rid me of crow's feet and blubbery thighs, he was very professional which, in light of my situation, felt a bit compassionate. He talked of reconstruction surgery as if it were an everyday occurrence, which for him it probably was.

After discussing our options, having me stand and display my stomach and rear-end to substantiate the choice of whether implants would be used or tissue from my body, I was whisked away for my first nudie shot. (Well, that sounds a bit risqué and out of character.) Actually, I stood in a narrow room with both white and black walls, and rotated from side to side in order to provide a before surgery picture of my breasts so that when they put me back together again I wouldn't be mismatched like Humpty Dumpty. After my Kodak moment I returned to the room with my husband, where the whole scenario felt a bit odd. It was funny though, how we had both become accustomed to other people seeing and feeling my breast - not something I could ever have imagined before my diagnosis.

We talked some more with the plastic surgeon and felt again that we were in good hands for post-surgery reconstruction. The plan, with a faint asterisk, incase radiation was necessary, was to reconnect with him a couple weeks after surgery and begin reconstruction two months after my mastectomy. Before saying goodbye he left us with one very important instruction: "Tell the surgeon to save skin!" He repeated this again and again adding, in case we were unsure, "You have breast cancer not skin cancer."

On the way home Mike and I chatted about the experience. Mike seemed proud that I didn't have enough cushion in either my stomach or my rear end to reconstruct a breast without the use of an implant. I begged to differ but I suppose the surgeon was the expert. So the plan, which we always love to have, was to start with an expander, a crescent shaped balloon like thing that would be surgically placed under my remaining chest tissue and gradually inflated with saline fluid. Once it was filled to a desired volume, which basically meant my chest wall had stretched to the size of my perfect new breast, the expander would be replaced with an implant. There would be some tedious finishing touches and then, voila! I would be back to normal and maybe even a bit improved.

The good news was that it would be a gradual growth. It would be like puberty all over again, but a bit faster and no zits. I didn't have to worry about going from flat to double D over night. They weren't going to slip a Dolly P in me and send me on my way. We could advise, "A little bigger, a little bigger, a little bigger, perfect!" After all the things I didn't have control over, this felt pretty good. We were pleased and optimistic.

WINK

Chapter Eleven

Tick tock, tick tock... the time kept creeping along and finally the day arrived. We said our goodbyes to the kids and my mom, and then Mike escorted me to the hospital. We went to the check-in desk, where they sent me to the lab, where they sent me to the mammography area, where they sent me to the diagnostic area and advised me to take a seat. I was a bit unnerved by all the chaos but remained confident that everything was going to be just fine. Mike and I each had a book in hand. He, *Angels and Demons* and me, *The Lightning Thief,* a book I had promised Marcus I would read because he loved it so much. To our dismay we discovered neither of us could focus enough to read. Instead, we entertained ourselves with various games on his iPhone. Finally my name was called and it was time to start the day's journey. Phase one was a radioactive injection used to locate my sentinel nodes; the surgeon would be extracting one or two of them to determine if my lymph system had been invaded by the little cancer buggers. We were told it could take twenty minutes or it could take two hours for the lymph nodes to show up on the x-ray machine. Hurry up and wait seemed to be a recurring theme; however, being the compliant person I am, my lymph nodes showed up in twenty-five minutes. X-rays were taken, and I was on to the surgical waiting room.

As time passed, more and more family members arrived to show their support. I felt like I had my own entourage. Our mingling came to a halt when the nurse took me to prepare me for surgery.

First she had me stand on the scale. It was a metric calculation, which didn't leave me begrudging how many sweets I shouldn't have eaten the week before. (As if fretting over how much I weighed was worthy of a thought before going in for mastectomy surgery, but, I did find it comical that I weighed less than three digits.) After my weigh-in I changed into my darling robe. I couldn't remember whether the opening went in the front or the back so I opted for the front. I climbed in my hospital bed, was asked a bazillion health questions and my IV was started. My reward was a fancy paper blanket that hooked up to some kind of hot air heating unit. It kept me warm while my visitors returned for their final goodbyes.

The surgeon came in and talked to Mike and me about the surgery. Despite running the risk of sounding like a loony, and embarrassing Mike, I asked, "If all the prayers and alternative healing I have been doing for the past month worked, and there actually isn't any cancer, would you know that when you open me up?" Maybe she had heard questions like this before or maybe it was just part of her delightful demeanor, but with-out judgment or hesitation she responded, "No, pathology will evaluate the tissue. We will be going in for a left mastectomy." So I guess a surgeon doesn't just open you up, see a specific color of non-desirable tissue and cut along the dotted lines like a seamstress cutting out a pattern. I let her know I just had to ask, and I was thinking to myself, "No biggie. It's just a surgery taking out something that could be replaced with something bigger and better." We discussed the issue of saving skin, though not at the risk of leaving behind any cancer, if in fact it was there. She had already spoken with the plastic surgeon and was aware of his desires. (Who would have ever imagined that I would be such a topic of conversation?) She signed the upper quadrant of my left chest, to confirm we were both on the same page as to where the surgery would be taking place, and then she bid her farewell until the operating room.

The next visitor to my pre-surgical corner was the anesthesiologist. Truly the only anxiety I had for the whole procedure was being put to sleep, a true testament to my desire for control. I would much rather watch the surgery, numb to the bone of course, than wake up and have it all over. Unfortunately that wasn't an option. The anesthesiologist discussed with Mike and me the process of putting me to sleep. He explained that prior to administering the actual sleeping medication he would give me a precursor so I wouldn't even feel the medication going in. He seemed very confident that I would do fine. I said my goodbyes to Mike and I was on my way. I arrived in the operating room and, as requested by Karli, I noticed that it wasn't like the operating rooms seen on her favorite television medical drama series. It lacked the hustle and bustle and it wasn't cluttered with an overabundance of equipment as typically seen on the various emergency room shows. The next thing I knew I was awake in the recovery room. Just like that, the whole thing was over. A nurse was by my side, filling out paperwork and getting me ice as I lingered somewhere between oblivion and consciousness. When I was alert enough, I was wheeled in my bed past the surgery waiting room to pick up my husband and then on to a hospital room. I barely remember the afternoon, falling in and out of sleep. I knew Mike was by my side, but I was too tired to stay awake.

Finally, by early evening I became alert enough to have a conversation and visitors. Our children were eager to drop in, and I was just as excited to reassure them that everything had gone smoothly. They stayed for a short while, but long enough to remind me that I wasn't the center of the universe. Their sibling rivalry was alive and well.

Mike stayed the night with me, scrunched on a corner couch, comforting me with his love and compassion. Nurses came in throughout the night to check my vitals, ensuring that if Mike couldn't get a good night's sleep then neither could I. But none of that mattered because the surgery was over and everything was going to be good from here on out.

I received my walking papers first thing in the morning. After gaining an understanding of the tubes protruding from the ace bandage that wrapped around my bodice, and how to care for them, Mike and I gathered our belongings and were quickly on our way.

Once home I was quarantined to my bedroom by both my mom and Mike. Directed to climb in bed and do nothing, I complied as I had promised ahead of time. Still tired from the lack of sleep, and perhaps the medications too, I continued to nod off. They waited on me hand and foot constantly refreshing my ice-pack and making sure beverages were always an arm's length away.

For the next few days I was treated as royalty. My life of leisure consisted of reading books, strolling around the house and the neighborhood, and sipping cold lemonade. I was excused from household chores and cooking meals. I continued to drink green tea rather than coffee, to solidify that the alternative efforts I had made had certainly helped cure me of the cancer. My duties as a patient were comprised of emptying my surgical drain, not showering and finding appropriate things to wear.

The latter was the hardest. I had mastered the sponge bath technique, and my mom and daughter were gracious enough to wash my hair for me. I thought I had been prepared for post-surgery dress by purchasing a special camisole equipped with drain holders and pockets to hold pads designed to falsify the breast which had been removed. The only problem was that although it fit before surgery, it was made out of Lycra and impossible to get on with the limited range-of-motion I had after surgery. Against my better judgment I convinced myself that it was made as a post-surgical undergarment and I needed to wear it. Standing in my bedroom, I contorted myself so that I was able to get the body of the camisole on.

I managed one arm through the opening, but in an attempt to get the other arm in; I could neither continue on nor back out. Panic overcame me as I felt stuck in the contraption. I called for Karli who came to my rescue and helped me out of it. I still had my ace bandage on and that was going to have to suffice for the remainder of my journey.

For the first couple of days after surgery my attire consisted of Mike's button-up shirts. They were convenient and comfortable. Then I was given some more appropriately sized ladies button-up shirts that looked better but weren't really my style with their Hawaiian floral theme. I soon realized that zip-up sweatshirts, with pockets, suited me best. They allowed me to put a drain in one pocket and my numbing drip in the other. This prevented me from continuously, absentmindedly walking away leaving them behind to fall to the floor and tug at my skin. Fortunately both tubes were securely attached and held down by the ace bandage that remained in place twenty-four hours a day. I hadn't caused permanent damage by my carelessness but I worried that they would eventually come loose if I didn't learned how to keep better track of them.

Having mastered keeping my tubes to myself around the house, I decided to venture out with my family to see a dance recital. I had become even more inventive for the outing by packing my paraphernalia in a large, over-the-shoulder bag. It was a fairly dark auditorium so I didn't feel too self-conscious. Feeling even more adventurous, the next day I went to my son's school to watch his field day. This time I discovered that, despite the fashion faux pas, a fanny pack was much more convenient to hide the tubes in. A true inventor at heart, I was pleased with my innovations.

WINK

Chapter Twelve

Five days after surgery Mike and I returned to my doctor's office. She would check the incision sight and convey the pathology results to us. I was feeling good and was sure we would get a standard clean bill of health allowing me to proceed with reconstruction in just under two months.

It was a familiar routine: check-in, be escorted to an examining room, have a seat and wait. As usual, the doctor's friendly voice rang in just moments later. She had the pathology report in hand, with a patient copy for me. First the good news: the sentinel nodes were clear, negative for any cancer, which meant it truly was in-situ and it hadn't spread anywhere else in my body. my internal voice was screaming, "Ya-hoo-e!" or at least some form of the celebratory word. Then the tone in her voice seem to change a bit, alluding to the fact that perhaps the rest of the news wasn't exactly what we had hoped for. She went on to explain that although she had been able to extract the entire span of the cancer, which measured 6 cm, the margins were less than 1mm. Good news and bad news seemed to be a recurring cycle. You have breast cancer but a good kind; we got it but the margins are too small.

Originally there had been a minute possibility of me having radiation because the calcifications were located so close to my chest wall. For this reason I couldn't have the expander put in at the time of my mastectomy, but I had gotten my hopes up that it wouldn't come to fruition. It wasn't exactly denial, but I had believed that 1) I didn't really have cancer; 2) if by chance I did have cancer, I had cured it with more level headed thinking and alternative treatments despite the time constraints; and 3) I certainly wouldn't

72

need radiation. Now I was being told that since I was so young they wanted to make absolutely sure that no little critters were hiding, and in fact I would need seven weeks of radiation.

Radiation isn't like chemo, with all the monstrous side effects, but what it does do is kill all the tissue that is being radiated. For a woman wanting reconstruction that changes everything. It doesn't make it impossible but it certainly delays the process at least six months and requires an additional surgery to take tissue from the back, known as the latissimus dorsi flap, and move it to the front. This positively was not the news we had been anticipating.

The doctor then explained that she had a call into the pathologist and radiation oncologist because there was a chance that she could increase the margins by doing a simple surgery, removing some of the skin that was spared for the original reconstruction plan. With that she examined my incision, which I had no desire to look at, removed the numbing pack but left the

73

drain and redressed me with a brand new ace bandage. She said she would call me to confirm, but I needed to make an appointment for surgery again in two days.

Mike and I shared a few tears as we left in disbelief that I really had had cancer and now I really needed treatment. Up until this point I just thought of it as a surgery, not a disease. I was angry that I gave up coffee for a month and had been foolish enough to believe I could cure myself with alternative healing. I was upset for having been so vain - in requesting to 'save skin' and quite frankly, felt a little hoodwinked by the whole thing. This had all clearly spiraled out of my control. I planned to go home and drink an entire pot of coffee, never mind a cup.

After some time of bereavement I tried to regain my positive disposition and nonchalant attitude. I thought to myself, *this wasn't the worst thing that could have happened. The lymph nodes were clean and that is all that really mattered.*

Not letting the disappointment of my diagnosis get the better of me I continued to attend customary events. While I was at Marcus' end-of-the-school-year party the dreaded call came in. A quick shift occurred from my being entertained by the architectural talents of fourth-graders and how much whip cream and candy toppings they can construct on top of one scoop of ice-cream to the angst of receiving confirmation that I would be having outpatient surgery in less than forty-eight hours. Unlike the original surgery requiring an overnight stay, I was advised that this time I would basically be in and out before noon.

Returning to the group I tried to readjust my internal disappointment so that it more closely matched my outwardly blasé portrayal of the second surgery. I told myself it was no big deal, to suck it up and quit being such a baby. *Get over yourself!* my internal voice cried out and yet, for some reason I was feeling the need to wallow in self-pity. Here I was again, acting like the young child that didn't get her way. It was not an appealing characteristic, and I welcomed the day it would all be over.

D-day arrived once again. I was the first surgery of the day so we had to check in at 5:45 a.m. This time they didn't lead me all over the hospital. They entered my personal data into the computer, gave me an ID bracelet and took me to the surgical waiting room. Shortly thereafter I was taken through the familiar double doors and led right to the scale. The novelty had worn off and I found no amusement in the experience. I was taken to a pre-operation cubical and given a gown to change into. I was directed to take everything off which posed a problem for me this time. I had been wearing my ace bandage for a week straight, aside from my check-up, and had no intention of having a looky-loo just before going into surgery. Fortunately the nurse was able to help me transition with-out my catching a glimpse. I lay on the bed under a sheet, this time without any warm air to comfort me. That luxury must only come with the deluxe overnight package.

The nurse asked me all the same questions I had been asked the previous week and then set out to begin the IV process. I informed her that I had been told that I had rolly veins. Grateful for the information, she cautiously proceeded to stick me with a needle. Unfortunately, even with the warning, the attempt was unsuccessful and she had to try again. Moving from the crevice of my arm to my inner wrist she readied me for another try. Just then her cell phone rang. She answered it, spoke briefly, hung up and then explained that it was her daughter checking in; for the first time she was home alone getting ready for school. My motherly compassion kicked in as I thought of my own children at home getting ready for school with my mom. Back to business, she cleaned the selected IV spot, eased the needle in and with pain and discomfort climbing up my arm, she again had to withdraw the needle. At this point tears were starting to seep from my eyes. I was feeling unsure and pathetic.

Just a week prior, I had been in the same room confident and poised for a successful endeavor. This time I felt like the cowardly lion, losing ground with every poke. Things hadn't gone the way I wanted earlier in the week and they certainly weren't going well now. The third IV attempt, in the back of my hand, was a success. Since I was all prepped for surgery Mike was able to reunite with me in my pre-surgical 'suite'. He arrived, worried to see I had been crying. I had lost my positive footing and didn't know how to reestablish it. Mike reminded me that everything was going to be fine and that we would get through this, a motto I had come to know all too well. He was being strong for me but obviously felt so much of my pain. We deflected our sadness with round two of *Who Wants to be a Millionaire* on his iPhone followed by a game of Scrabble.

After a while someone came and told us that my surgery time was delayed because an emergency surgery had required our operating room. I didn't know whether to laugh or to cry. Was this a sign that I should just get up and walk out? That's what I wanted to do. I just wasn't feeling up to surgery at the moment. Obviously that wasn't an option, so I found strength in knowing that whatever emergency surgery was taking place it was certainly more life-threatening than mine. It was the kick I needed to get refocused. I had regained my composure and was prepared to find a word, among my Scrabble tiles, that would gain me some much-needed points.

When the operating room had cleared out my doctor came to talk with us and make her signature mark. Even she said it was a bit redundant seeing as how it would be hard to operate on the wrong breast, but it was standard procedure. She left and the anesthesiologist appeared. This time I had no fear of going under, probably because I feared so many other things, but the anesthesiologist did his due diligence of keeping me informed. He told me, since it was going to be such a short surgery I wouldn't get the

79

three course meal of medications and that I wouldn't be injected with the anesthetic until I was in the operating room. Knowing what to expect I said goodbye to Mike and was rolled away, bed and all.

I think the anesthesiologist was used to people being a little freaked out, like I was last time - either that or my nurse had expressed how I had been crying like a baby, because he did a fabulous job of communicating to me exactly what was going on. He even slowed to show me the full operating room schedule for the day and commented on the normalcy of people having surgery.

We arrived in my operating room. This time I was able to truly look around the room and make note of the differences and similarities between this room and those on TV. I felt proud that I would be able to clearly differentiate the two for Karli when I got home, as the space I occupied reminded me more of the white room with oopa loompas in Charlie and the Chocolate Factory than any of the operating rooms shown on television.

The anesthesiologist pointed out the boom box and noted that some doctors now listen to their iPods during surgery. My rolling bed was then placed alongside a hard table covered with a sheet. I scooted over to what was now my operating bed. Lying flat, the anesthesiologist had me hold an oxygen mask over my nose and mouth while he stuck various monitors on me. None of this was even remotely familiar from the previous week. After I was all hooked up and ready to go, he advised me that I may feel a sharp shooting pain in my arm as the medicine moved through my veins. Still commentating on every detail, he reassured me that it would pass in a few seconds. Just as I was about to inform him that yes, in fact I could feel the pain and report it wasn't going away, he started counting down from ten, nine. Then I remembered our friend, who had survived cancer just the year before, challenging me to fight to stay alert despite the drugs - and then I was out. I don't even think I heard the anesthesiologist say eight.

The next thing I knew they were wheeling me out of the operating room into recovery. I was awake much quicker this time. A nurse was there to greet me but was busily writing notes. Rather than taking me to a hospital room I was moved to a sitting room. I changed back into my clothes and had juice and crackers. Mike rejoined me and sure enough we were home before noon. It was all over and I survived.

I took it easy for the next couple of days. Continuing to experiment with new inventions, I discovered that I could string a long necklace through a loop on my breast drain and have it dangle at my midsection. Though it made me look a little pregnant, the furthest thing from my mind, I no longer had to fight to hide tubing when I went out and about and worry that I would scare the children at the bus stop with tubes of bodily fluid dangling at my side. I was beginning to feel more at ease since I had gotten better about concealing my recently acquired possessions.

I revisited my surgeon a few days later where the new pathology report came back clean, which was to be expected. She removed the drain leaving me feeling like a free woman, then wrapped a new ace bandage around me for comfort and told me I was free to shower. She advised that as long as I didn't over extend myself too much I could go about my normal routine. Before I left, my surgeon gave me the single assignment of calling to schedule an appointment with the radiation oncologists.

WINK

Chapter Thirteen

One would think that I would race home and take a shower, an event I hadn't experienced for twelve days. The original thought of going so long without bathing was a bit repulsive. However, the revolting thoughts of grunge had been replaced with a much stronger feeling of apprehension for what I would expose once naked. I wondered just how disgusting I would look once I uncovered my wound.

I busied myself with everyday tasks, which at this point included making appointments. Summer brings reprieve even for doctors and with vacations at their height I couldn't get in to see the oncologist for two weeks. I welcomed the break from medical care. Knowing I was on my own for a while I had the courage to venture into the bathroom and tend to my needs.

Taking off my sweatshirt, I stood looking at the all too familiar ace bandage. Though I didn't feel any pain where the breast had been removed, it felt strange, like your lip after having a Novocain shot at the dentist: you know it's there but can't really feel it. I tugged at the Velcro strip and slowly began to unwind the wrap. I wanted the ability to quickly cover up if it was so grotesque that I couldn't stomach the sight. Round and round the wrap went. It felt as long as a red carpet leading up to a royal court, only this would not be even remotely as enchanting. Nearing the end, the bandage dropped from my body, no longer held down by the overlay. Keeping my head up, I used my peripheral vision to scan the area. Deciding that is wasn't as revolting as I had anticipated, I gradually side stepped into full view of the mirror.

Looking at the reflection staring back at me I realized not much had changed. Sure, the

85

surgery had affected one small area that would forever be altered, but quite frankly a smile came over me. As I gazed at the mirror image of my naked body, a configuration that once consisted of the typical female anatomy, one that had never gained too much of a personal assessment, now stared back as a winking face - not the reaction I had anticipated. Perhaps it was a bit peculiar, especially since I had never viewed my breast as eyes with a bellybutton mouth just inches below, but somehow my body now had a cheerful face that was secretly mine. Maybe it had been all the family gatherings of performing the Saturday Night Live character "Mr. Chin," but I was pleasantly surprised that not only did the mastectomy site not send me into a tail spin of depression; I could actually smile about it.

I hopped into the shower where the warm water washed across my body. I still had limited range of motion with my arm from the sentinel node biopsy, but I welcomed the challenge of lathering from head to toe. I had never felt so clean. I rewrapped the ace bandage, which had become my comfort blanket, and got dressed.

The next two weeks quickly brought normalcy to my life. Without my drain to add volume to my chest, my asymmetry became more apparent. Surprisingly, I hadn't ventured back to the mall to replace my unsuccessful post-surgery camisole with a fitted bra and prosthetics. Instead I had started my period, so grateful it had come after the surgeries and with all the necessary feminine protection basics handy, my creative instincts kicked in and I constructed my own breast pad. I felt like a pre-adolescent girl stuffing her bra to the point of satisfaction. After a week of using a pad I discovered ankle socks worked just as well with-out the cotton residue.

WINK

Chapter Fourteen

Just as my life was beginning to take its familiar shape the dreaded day arrived to meet with the radiation oncologist. Heading into the appointment "the plan" was to have seven weeks of radiation to make sure I was cured, being so young and all.

We arrive at the reception desk where I was greeted by name despite having only been to the office once before. This was the same office my sister had accompanied me to just a month prior and been extremely impressed by the doctor. Mike and I sat in the waiting area reading some funny stories on one of his iPhone applications, a continuous source of entertainment for us, until we were called back to an examination room. The nurse recorded my vitals, debriefed us a bit about the 'mapping' process for radiation and then moved us to a different room to await the oncologist. A short time passed as Mike and I reminisced about my naive response to the doctor's question of why I thought I had gotten breast cancer. Mike and I joked, adding more absurd reasons, and then we heard a knock just before the door opened.

I had given Mike a preliminary run-down on what to expect from the doctor: a confident, self-assured man who was very knowledgeable. After introductions the doctor asked how my psychological demeanor was. I responded that all had been pretty good despite the setback of needing radiation and with that we delved into a highly unexpected conversation on the lack of a substantial necessity for radiation. Though the decision was left entirely up to Mike and me, the conversation consisted of debriefings from top doctors in the country specializing in Ductal Carcinoma In-situ (DCIS) with whom the oncologist had discussed my case. (I must say I felt honored)   No one seemed to think that the benefits outweighed the risks for radiation.

Mike and I were shocked into disbelief. We never imagined that we would be walking out of the office with-out numerous radiation appointments scheduled. It took a few moments to register but then almost in celebratory unison we realized reconstruction was no longer going to be months away.

We thanked the doctor for the great news, shook hands and agreed that a random encounter at Costco would be more welcomed than another meeting in his office. Mike and I left astounded by the news. It had been what we had wanted right from the start but disappointment had set in after the mastectomy when we realized that plans changed. Now we were back on track, reunited with our original plan and we couldn't have been happier. Mike said he truly didn't think he had ever cried from happiness before, as the tears welled in his eyes. I started back tracking and thinking of all the coffee I had been drinking and the thank you' s I hadn't sent out yet for all the flowers, meals and prayers that had been provided.

I called my mom and daughter, who were together, to tell them the good news. Among the absolute joy my daughter said, "Maybe all that voodoo stuff you did worked." "Yes, I am guessing it did," I answered.

After a rush of phone calls and emails, Mike and Karli gathered their belongings for a scheduled trip to the summer camp our children attended about sixty miles away to prepare for an upcoming camp open house. I planned to join them the following night, closer to the true visitor's day, since Marcus was in session at camp and I didn't want to inflict undue homesickness upon him. Bantering about something with Mike as he was about to leave, I said to him, "You better watch it or it just may end up a 'B' cup." Never one to give ultimatums, I just couldn't resist the temptation to celebrate that the choice was with-in reach again. With smiles extending from ear to ear, goodbyes were exchanged.

I hadn't anticipating feeling the need to celebrate. The whole cancer thing had become quite mundane and uninteresting. I was relieved when my mother-in-law called and declared a celebration was in order. Who better to celebrate with? After all, she was the one who saved my life by the constant reminders of getting a mammogram. It was a delightful evening; good food, good company and good times. It was a terrific ending to an amazing day.

WINK

Chapter Fifteen

The next day, with the rest of the family away, I joined my father and his wife for an afternoon lunch. Though we get together at various times through-out the year, it is mostly for his doctor appointments (as he has been battling lung cancer for just over two years) or holidays and birthdays and always with the kids. This was the first time I had ever actually met them for a meal and conversation with-out the numerous distractions having the kids along creates. I'm not sure of the reason I had made the plans. Maybe I was feeling guilty since my own doctor's appointments had gotten in the way of me attending his, maybe it was because of all the times he said, "I wish we could see more of you and the kids," and I nonchalantly replied, "I know." Always casually adding, "It is so hard with everyone's schedules," or maybe this time it was because I was feeling that I was cured and he wasn't.

I had experienced cancer without too much collateral damage, and though there are many worse off than my dad, he hadn't been as fortunate as I had. Despite the doctor giving him a prognosis of six months to live he continued trying various chemo treatments that gave him an array of side effects. They ranged from swelling all over the body to bruising to watery red eyes, and these were just a few of the visual ones. I also knew he had a slew of them that were too private to openly discuss. Cancer ignites a diverse response in those diagnosed, and my dad and I clearly represent that reality. Though we both had set out certain to beat the disease, our approaches had been completely different.

I was pleasantly surprised when my dad greeted me at the door. He looked the best I had seen him for ages. All of the issues I previously mentioned were gone. His hair was full and aside from a bit of coughing, which had been a symptom for as long as I could remember, he looked pretty darn good. We sat at their home for a bit as I gave the run-down on the family and then we headed out to lunch.

It was a nice sunny day so they chose an upbeat restaurant on the waterfront. We sat outside on the deck feeling the warmth of the sun on our faces with a plethora of scenery to entertain us. Conversations fluttered in and out of each of our cancer experiences, the kids and random bits of trivia. After the leisurely lunch we made our way back to their house, and I left shortly thereafter. It had been less awkward than usual and a rather pleasant experience.

On my way home I wondered to myself what had been different. Suddenly I realized that I had been gaining a sense of peace over the past few months. Though I would never truly understand the way in which I was raised, I was accepting that my father had done the best he could, a broken youth himself. I was letting go of the hurt from childhood and was replacing it with gratitude to him for having given me life. I had become thankful for the good things and had let go of the bad. Had I not spent years of counseling to break the silence and make sure family secrets weren't passed on to my children? Harboring resentment contradicted that growth.

In receiving my diagnosis I realized I had been making myself sick by consciously and unconsciously holding on to the hurt. In her book, *Heal Your Body*, Louise L. Hay suggested new thought patterns for those suffering from cancer. She recommended we "lovingly forgive and release all of the past." She suggested choosing to fill our world with joy and to love and approve of ourselves. Though I had aspired time and time again to gain the strength to accomplish this, it seemed as though this time I had actually reached some success. I had a new sense of calm about me and it reflected in the outing with my dad.

Free of cancer thanks to surgery and free of cancer thanks to loving thoughts and prayers, I was feeling less stress than I could remember having for a long time.

WINK

Chapter Sixteen

The afternoon rolled on, bringing me closer to reuniting with Mike and Karli at camp, and the chance to see Marcus for the first time in eleven days. When I saw Marcus he greeted me with a huge smile, a hug and the very loving words, "I am so happy to hear that you don't have to have radiation." He never ceased to amaze me with his compassion, which was always far beyond his age. Throughout my stay at camp, in between introductions to counselors and new friends, Marcus repeatedly conveyed his joy about my not needing radiation. I could feel how genuinely happy he was. I felt a bit of relief that, although he was staying at camp for another ten days, his heart was a little less burdened with worry and a bit more carefree.

Continuing my walk on cloud nine I decided I would treat my newly healed body with a bit more respect. I vowed to exercise more and eat better. As advised, I made an appointment to meet with yet another oncology doctor about Tamoxifen, a breast cancer prevention drug. In addition to this meeting I anxiously awaited my next appointment with the plastic surgeon to prepare for my reconstruction.

A month and a half after surgery I met with the doctor in the cancer center at the hospital I had frequented for my cancer care. Not really knowing what to expect, I was simply complying with my surgeon and the radiation oncologist to discuss the benefits of Tamoxifen - the least I could do after all they had done for me.

Once in the examination room I was greeted by a petite, extremely young looking gal with short black hair and dark rimmed glasses with both M.D. credentials and a Ph. D. She conveyed her deep understanding of my case as she conferred facts about my procedures and pathology, referring to a full sheet of hand written notes. She was obviously very knowledgeable of not only me but cancer in general. She honored me by acknowledging that all the choices that lay in my future were mine to make but gently added that considering the size of my DCIS and the mention of a non-remarkable 5mm area seen on my right side in my MRI, doing nothing would not necessarily be a good choice.

We discussed Tamoxifen, its side effects and its limitations. I thought of the hassles and the costs even though, fortunately, my insurance had been, rather generously, footing the bill. I asked if a preventative right mastectomy was a better choice than the Tamoxifen. She said I had time to entertain the idea and ponder the thought with my husband, but she did advise that although a preventative mastectomy would substantially reduce my chances of getting breast cancer in my remaining breast, Tamoxifen would be more helpful in seeking out a straggling cell, in the off chance that one might have escaped somewhere else in my body.

Having decided that talking things over with my husband would be the best decision, we bid farewell with the assurance I would call back to inform her of my choice. Not loving the idea of taking a drug for five years that has the side effects of menopause, weight gain and forgetfulness, I delayed the conversation until we could be rejuvenated by the plastic surgeon. A couple days later we met with the plastic surgeon, scheduled to have the expander put in just after the kids went back to school, and welcomed the reality that this would all soon be a distant memory.

Mike and I discussed the Tamoxifen and decided that, just as he does his daily shot to potentially ward off the advancement of his M.S., I would take Tamoxifen for the same reason but for breast cancer. In keeping my right breast we also decided that, since so many factors seemed unclear, I would have the genetic testing done. Contrary to my typical head in the sand health care theory, knowledge is power.   I made an appointment for the following month, as I wasn't ready yet to give up my joyful delusion that everything was back to normal.

WINK

Chapter Seventeen

In an effort to maintain my mirage of normalcy I decided it was time to venture back in to the lingerie section of a local department store for a bra fitting and insert. It had been nearly two months since surgery, and although I had become very comfortable wearing sports bras and stuffing socks in them, I had grown tired of sporting a racer back look with everything I put on. Once at the store I felt silly and a little overindulgent seeing as how I would begin reconstruction in under a month, but the gal I had scheduled an appointment with said we could just try a few things and see what I thought.

How quickly we trick ourselves into thinking we look fine. Putting on a bra for the first time in months I discovered I was more of a woman than I remembered. I had become accustomed to the look that the sports bra conveyed and thought I wore it well. Once it was no longer squished between Lycra my breast perked up and welcomed the soft padded bra that gave it form. The gal provided me a smooth gel like "swimform" to insert into my empty breast cup to help balance me out and hold the bra in place. Evaluating the image in the mirror, I was horrified that I had believed I looked somewhat normal with-out all these fancy undergarments. Who had I been kidding? Obviously, only myself.

Happy with my purchase I went home and modeled it for my mother. She was so sweet to show such enthusiasm. When my husband got home I asked him how come he hadn't told me I had been looking so ridiculous. He simply responded that he thought I was just okay with everything and didn't mind the look. I can't blame him for his assumption. My wardrobe speaks little of fashion and days go by where I am lucky if I put on lipstick and a hair band but little did he know I thought I hadn't needed the expensive replacements because I had successfully created the desired look on my own. Just as one who gains weight over the years and doesn't recognize it until one day comparing pictures, I had foolishly deceived myself into believing I looked as normal as I had prior to surgery. Though only a few months had passed it was a progression from surgery, to an ace bandage, to a sports bra. I was developing right before my eyes.

I was happy to have breasts back, though a little apologetic to my surviving breast for having squished it for so long. I liked that I could ease into yet another stage in my enhancement as I disrobed at night and carefully placed my gel prosthetic back in its box. It was nice taking baby steps to growth. Soon enough they would be a permanent part of me, and surely less saggy than the current 41 year-old one.

Summer continued to quickly pass. Marcus returned from camp and Karli ventured off to camp. A sense of calmness had replaced the turmoil of the past few months. My mom went on a much needed vacation, a cruise with her sister, and my sister and her family came to stay with us. It was great having the kids together to play and some adult time to chat.

During this same week my dad received some good news about his lung cancer. The tumors had shrunk on his last scan. He had been battling the disease for more than two years, already longer than they had initially projected despite a few times having been given just six months to live. Unfortunately, the good news was shadowed by the reality that a tumor had grown on his hip and he needed to start another round of radiation. As with my cancer journey, there was often both good news and bad news.

The weeks went by fast. My sister left and the Northwest's record-breaking heat wave subsided. I had run out of reasons to prolong the start of Tamoxifen any longer. Having had the prescription filled weeks prior, I routinely moved the white pharmacy bag from the kitchen counter to the bathroom shelf to my bedside table and had finally come to the conclusion it was time to start my five-year endeavor. I opened the childproof lid, took out the little white pill and swallowed. It was rather uneventful. I didn't sprout a tail, didn't plump four sizes or become overwhelmed with a sweaty sensation. However, I have taken to hula hooping at night and watching more carefully what I eat in an attempt to avoid the possible side effects.

WINK

Chapter Eighteen

Moving right along, it had been nice to conquer this breast cancer thing in stages: stereotactic biopsy, check; MRI, check; EKG, check; Mastectomy, check; additional skin surgery, check; Tamoxifen, check. With the mysterious event of reconstruction still looming on the horizon, I decided I would finally accept the offer to visit with my friend who had previously gone through breast cancer. She had been a confidant to me on many occasions during the past few months and now, with two weeks until my final destination, I hoped I was ready to hear the rest of the story. She had a friend who had just finished a year on the cancer conquest who was willing to share her experiences with me as well.

The three of us arranged to meet at the local coffee shop. I had come a long way from my forty plus years of modesty. Now I was able to discuss breasts, or the lack of, over a venti decaf non-fat latte. After introductions were made, the conversations quickly flowed into our stories. I was intrigued by what I heard. I learned how each of our experiences had been so different, a lumpectomy, a mastectomy, and a double mastectomy.

They talked of how just a year earlier they had sat at the same coffee shop with another breast cancer survivor who openly shared her story. The tables had turned, and rather than listening to stories of survivorship, my friend's friend was now a survivor herself. During the past year this gal had lived through three major surgeries, the double mastectomy where she also had the expanders put in, the removal of the expanders and replacement with implants and most recently the application of nipples. She was paying it forward, uncovering the mystery for me, just as someone had done for her.

She shared with me her reasons for choosing silicone versus saline and gave me a better understanding of the pain that accompanied expanders. Wondering if the pain was similar to an achy body after excessive exercise or more like what one might feel if her hand was slammed in the door of a car I got the feeling it was somewhere in between. I decided it would be okay to stick with my plan of Tylenol rather than the prescription drugs, but would have the hard stuff on hand in case of an emergency.

Though the process seemed complicated and time consuming, the end result appeared to be worthy of all the hassle. She even provided me a firsthand peek. I was pleasantly surprised that it looked quite natural. I didn't linger and stare for the sake of both of our comfort. It would have been a sheer disappointment to any man with a wild imagination watching three women entering a single stall bathroom, but it did give me a clearer picture of what was in store for me.

As I left the coffee shop amazed with the aesthetic appeal of the reconstruction I wondered to myself, after all the honest agony she had encountered, *Was this really worth it?* Going through all the distress just to have a blob put back on my chest. But those bewildering thoughts were quickly laid to rest after attending my husband's company picnic.

During the afternoon of fun, which included roaming from one bouncy toy to the next with my family, I looked down and noticed that I had been flaunting my lovely gel prosthetic for all to see. It had crept up to the neckline of my shirt. Just the reassurance I needed to answer my earlier, pondering question; *Yes, in fact it would be worth it.* And if that wasn't enough of a reason, the next week Marcus attended a week long baseball camp and I forgot to put in my insert altogether, three out of the five days.

As much as I would have liked to chalk it up to the side effects of Tamoxifin, I knew better; it was just my own forgetfulness. Though reconstruction wasn't going to be a picnic I was sure it would save me from many embarrassing encounters down the road.

WINK

Chapter Nineteen

With reconstruction beginning in a week there was one last cancer path to take: genetic testing. Since the doctor's consensus had been that I was a young, healthy woman who really had no reason for getting breast cancer, science would like to identify whether or not I was born with a mutated gene. My initial instinct was to forgo genetic testing. I am not one to look for problems. However, after learning that I may be able to unlock information for my daughter, my sister, and other relatives, I decided it would be similar to keeping the secret of the Rosetta Stone in the *Da Vinci Code*. Though I am not personally as intriguing as the mystery found between the pages of Dan Brown's book, I did feel a bit obligated to reveal the truth, if there was one. So with a change of heart I ventured in for the explanation of the test and a blood draw. The results would come in two weeks. If the test were to come back positive then my plastic surgeon would basically be on my payroll and Pandora's Box will have been opened. If the test came back negative, then science would conclude that it was just my dumb luck to have gotten breast cancer. After receiving all the information I needed I was led to the phlebotomy room where I hopped up in the chair, had rubber tubing tied around my right arm, squeezed a little squishy ball a few times and a technologist proceeded to fill a glass vile with my healthy-looking blood. She tucked the vile safely into a well-cushioned box to send to some fancy lab. With a Band-Aid on the crevice of my arm I went on my way with my fate in the hands of some unknown scientist. Genetic testing done, check.

The day before my reconstruction surgery I feverishly cleaned our home. Two weeks of no vacuuming and laundry had put me into what is typically identified among pregnant ladies as nesting. It was similar to what I had done prior to the mastectomy, only this time I had put my little gel prosthetic on the counter. I had learned that it was much easier to work without it, and since it was really for the sake of appearance, and there was no one around for me to be sporting my bodacious look for, I shed it for the mere convenience.

Sometime into my cleaning frenzy my mom returned home. Upon her arrival I stopped my labor intensive work to chat a bit. We had been talking briefly when she reached out to touch my gel prosthetic sitting on the counter, which I found to be a bit odd. It surprised me when she nearly jumped out of her skin - turns out she expected it to be hard. She thought it was an etched glass candy dish. The incident was hysterical and just one more reminder why it was a good thing I wouldn't need the assistance for much longer.

WINK

Chapter Twenty

With the house clean, the groceries stocked up and the family calendar filled in, it was time to begin my final journey. Mike had taken the day off of work to be my personal escort. Due to some unforeseen complications, unrelated to me, my surgery was postponed. First we waited at home and then at the doctor's office. For people of such precise programming as my husband and I, this generated some sense of restlessness. But, falling into routine we turned to his iPhone for entertainment. Shamefully laughing at people's stories on one of his applications and then moving on to a game of Trivial Pursuit, which I nearly came from behind to win, we kept entertained and occupied for quite some time.

Eventually we were called into the examination room where I was quickly whisked away for my preliminary bare breasted photos with the surgeon. This was a post-mastectomy shoot. I then returned to Mike in the examining room, along with the surgeon where he proceeded to fish through a variety of crescent-shaped plastic stencils until he found the right size to somewhat match my existing model. He asked if I had lost volume over the years and I said, "Yes, especially since my breast feeding days." Staying true to character, he merely replied, "You aren't saggy so much as just deflated. That will be easy to bring into symmetry with the new one, a little lift and a small implant."

Realizing I was just an anatomical body to him I continued to stand, naked from the waist up, occasionally looking at my husband as the surgeon traced the shape of the crescent on my chest. He drew straight lines, this way and that, using a ruler as a guide. With tattooing complete the surgeon left the room. I changed into my

117

beautiful gown and placed all my belongings in a plastic tote. The nurse came in, went over a few formalities, warned that I probably wouldn't remember much from the day and then advised it was time for goodbyes. With a quick exchange of a kiss I was escorted to the restroom and then the surgical room. Mike returned to the waiting room where he was advised to relax until being beckoned to retrieve me.

The surgical room was just like the white, sterile-looking room I remembered having my second breast surgery in. I climbed on the bed, had a little pillow placed under my knees and was covered with the warm air blowing blanked that I liked so much from my first stay at the hospital. I was hooked up to various machines, one with cuffs around my legs for constant circulation, plus an IV and a heart monitor too. The anesthesiologist was very friendly, and before I had even mentioned that I had roley veins the needle was in. I wanted to jump up and give her a big hug. That feeling quickly faded when the surgeon came in, the nurse said we were just about ready and the anesthesiologist advised she was administering the medicines. Like when I was in the hospital, I felt the pain shoot into my arm and then I was asleep. It all happened so fast.

Next thing I remembered the nurse was wheeling me to the car in a wheelchair. As we approached the car tears rolled down my face and in a confused state I admitted, I didn't know why I was crying. Feeling embarrassed I wiped the tears away. As she helped me into the car she casually explained the medication from surgery was causing the emotional outburst.

Once in the car and on our way home, I realize we were talking with Karli on the Bluetooth. Mike and I both reassured her that everything went well and Mike joked, "Tell mom what you had for lunch and something funny. She won't remember later." Karli confessed to me that she had popcorn chicken for lunch and the seniors made them go streaking in the halls at school. We arrived home and Mike gently got me into the house and in bed. By the time my mom arrived home with the kids they already knew I was doing well and simply wanted to know if I could remember what Karli had for lunch and what she did at school. I responded, "Popcorn chicken and streaking" and they disappointedly asked Mike, "When is she going to forget?" Determined not to forget I stuck to my plan of extra-strength Tylenol and lots of fluids rather than hard narcotics.

It was apparent from the aroma that swirled through the house that my mom had spent the day cooking. She had made corned beef, a family favorite, along with boiled vegetables and biscuits. I felt so bad when, despite it all being beautifully prepared everyone just grabbed a quick bite as they went on their way to the first Friday night high school football game of the season. I was not much better than the rest of the family, having resorted to being a bump on a log and not too interested in eating, but Mom reassured me that it was no problem. She told me that she remembered the days when she would prepare a family meal only to have everyone scatter here and there. She was a good sport, as always, and kept me good company for the evening. Mike did a great job of entertaining and chauffeuring the kids around. Day one of surgery was a success.

Day two was a lay-around day too. The weather had begun to change and fall was in the air. Rain fell and it made it a bit easier to lounge. Marcus went on a long awaited weekend trip with my mom to visit cousins and Karli meandered around with Mike and me. When she became sufficiently bored with us she decided to take her friends up on a sleepover invitation. After driving her to Timbuktu, Mike came and picked me up and we went to the movies. Though the movie itself wasn't too enthralling it was nice to get out of the house. I kept on the Tylenol regiment of two every four to six hours, keeping track not to exceed eight in a 24-hour period. I snoozed off and on and somehow during the night managed to let my refillable ice container, which I believed to be leak-proof, seep all over the bed.

By day three I was feeling much better and realized it would have been nice to have a good old-fashioned '70s- type tube top to wear underneath my sweatshirt. I didn't want to be contorting my arms through any holes but I had evolved from just wanting to go au-naturel. I settled on a tank top but still yearned for the fashion and support of days gone by. Alert and getting around with-out too much harassing from my family, I was able to evaluate the level of pain I had wondered about. If I had to describe it to the next victim of a tissue expander procedure I would equate it to the pain one might feel after a car accident or playing a game of tackle football. For me, it wasn't excruciating and my body only hurt when I moved, getting into and out of bed or on and off the couch. It was more like bruised ribs than labor pains. The Tylenol managed to keep the edge off, and rather quickly the pain began to subside.

I did have one unusual symptom. Some liquid pooled around my mid-section. It was a bit entertaining. I could stand in front of the mirror and just tap my side abdominals and see a little ripple effect. When I walked it jiggled. It was like I had a little hot water bottle tucked under my skin. I guess if I had been overly conscious about my weight it wouldn't have been so amusing but after what I had been through my weight was the least of my concerns. At Mike's request, I did check with the doctor. The doctor said it was nothing to worry about and that I was probably just retaining fluid, which made sense since I also had the pleasure of receiving a visit from "aunt flow". Though this eased my mind I would be lying if I said I wasn't a little freaked out about the whole thing. I hadn't planned for water retention and, according to the scale I had gained four pounds since surgery. I imagined by morning I would be at the ten pound marker and worried about it being a hematoma. Quickly squishing my thoughts of paranoia, I celebrated that it had been almost twelve hours since my last dose of Tylenol and I had no inclination of taking it again until closer to bed time. To help ease my mind I reminded myself that there would have been pain if it was something serious. With that I re-identified with my brave facade rather than the undesirable hypochondriac pretense and carried on business as usual.

Day turned into night and after sleeping off and on, I arose in the morning to the same body that went to bed. The bloating had not changed and it was a shower day. I carefully removed the outer surgical tape and gauze. My bodice had now transposed from the cheerful wink to a defective cartoon character. The wink had been converted to a semi-bulging round eye, the kind you might see drawn on either Homer or Bart Simpson in the comics, and the other side now appeared to be much droopier than I remembered. Thanks to the water retention, to add to my caricature, I now had side jowls too, like a Saint Bernard.

WINK

Chapter Twenty-one

I was a little baffled by the volume my expander already had. It looked close to its capacity, or at least to the final size that I had envisioned. It was way perkier than my existing side, which left me feeling a bit like an imposter. I was sure once I got used to it I would learn to appreciate it.

Feeling more emotional than usual I remembered the reasons I had become deflated. Fifteen years of parenting had taken the wind out of my pretentious ways and left me with the idea that saggy breasts were a mom's badge of honor. I wondered, *Am I loosing part of my identity in this transformation?* I'm not sure if it was the residual of the anesthetics or my elevated emotions due to

P.M.S., but I was surprised that, although I never felt the need to mourn the loss of my cancerous breast, I was suddenly filled with an unexpected sadness from my new development.

Up until this point it had all been something I could joke about. I was sure there had been plenty of light hearted "guy" exchanges to Mike of "How's your wife's rack coming along?" - a masculine way of asking how things were going with-out the emotional reality of the "C" word. I had even been a part of these very flippant comments among the doctors. They have made remarks, perhaps helping me to see the bright side of the whole breast cancer thing, reminding me that I would be exiting with a new and improved look. Heck - no surprise - Mike and I have even joked amongst ourselves, but now, somehow it was different.

The transformation was taking place and it was a bit scary. I had liked coming into my forties, arriving at the place in life where I wasn't supposed to care so much about what other people thought. I aspired to understand the world more deeply and gain knowledge beyond my miniscule horizons. Now, when I evolved with a new set of tatas, wasn't it like I was pretending that I cared about the deeper meaning in life when in actuality I cared about appearance? I stood to reflect the materialistic, outward appearance of shallowness rather than the profound importance of our existence.

It was a sad day for me but this too would pass. I knew there was so much more to being than my exterior; how important it is to accept myself for who I am behind the cover. This experience was a good lesson for me. Perhaps I had hidden behind a package of minimal make-up, bland clothing and nothing too extravagant. Maybe it was time to be more proactive in my approach to what mattered to me.

New day! Long before the days of shapeless breasts, parenthood did provide me with something much different. On this morning I was reminded of how the deflation occurred. I awoke to the engorged feeling one gets when breast milk comes in, shortly after delivering a new baby. With the pain medications from surgery clearly out of my system the inflated sensation was more tangible. The feeling accompanied me everywhere I went. I had no reprieve by an infant suckling or expressing milk at the nearest sink. I had to adjust to the bloated feeling and appreciate the ability to reminisce about early parenthood. The good news was I wouldn't have to experience cracked nipples or run the risk of mastitis as I did when I breast fed. Blessings come in all shapes and sizes.

WINK

Chapter Twenty-two

For the most part things had returned to normalcy. I focused on bigger and better things than my lingering medical predicament. However, I found myself thinking, *Only four more days until I get the results of the genetic testing.* It wasn't that I was debilitated with worry; it was more the ambiguity that bothered me. The wonder continuously passed in and out of my mind. I am a person that needs closure. Mike and I talk about this at great lengths. The open-endedness of arguments disturbs me. I can't let things go until I feel understood and sure that there is at least hope that the situation won't occur again. The loose ends of disease are haunting as well. Though I believe we control our outlook in life, and many directions our life goes based on our decisions, some of its bigger determinations are out of our hands. I reminded myself that there was no reason for me to get all freaked out about the test, especially since there really wasn't anything I could do about it. I couldn't have studied harder to influence whether I passed or failed. It was just a wait and see.

And then the phone rang…

Friday afternoon, on my way to pick-up Marcus from safety patrol my cell phone rang into my Bluetooth. "Hello," I answered and confirmed my identity. On the other end of the line a friendly voice revealed a name and reminded me that she was with the cancer center. She said, "I have the results from your genetic blood test." Three days early, and an entire weekend to be either sad or celebrate. "They are negative. You do not have the mutated gene," she revealed.

Very few times in my life could compete with the elation I felt upon receiving the news. "You are a God send!" I told her. "Thank you so much," I repeated over and over. I could tell she was happy to be the bearer of good news, and for a moment I tried to imagine what it would be like for her to call someone with the opposite results. I thanked her again and wished her a terrific weekend. Once I stopped driving I texted Mike, who was in a meeting at work, to give him the good news. Then I called my mom, who had gone to visit my sister.

"Guess what?" I quizzed her. Too impatient to wait for a response I immediately followed the question up with the answer, "I just got the results from the genetic testing." There was really no need to verbally convey the results; she could hear it in my voice. "It was negative!" I cheered. The joy in her voice, and the sounds that echoed in delight from my sister in the background, made for a moment of true celebration. It was a relief to us all. It was nice to share good news with no strings attached or a bad side to follow. It was just good solid data that confirmed that when I was done with reconstruction I was done with the nightmare. It had just been dumb luck for me to get breast cancer, and I was okay with that. I didn't have to wallow in self pity, having unknowingly passed on a mutated gene to my children. It was a time of sheer ecstasy for me.

WINK

Chapter Twenty-three

With each passing day my range of motion continued to improve. The tightness in my chest muscles was slowly loosening. The biggest problem I had was shaving under my arm. A cavern had been created by the crescent shaped expander protruding across my chest and slightly into my arm pit. Of course, I was unaware of the blind spot until I discovered a patch of hair that appeared to be creeping towards daylight when I applied deodorant one morning. Having always been a bit self-conscious of body hair I immediately called for Karli and pleaded with her to please help me shave my underarm. Naturally, she was happy to help and quickly put me at ease with the comfort of knowing I was clean-shaven.

Life was returning to normal. No lingering health mysteries, no more visits to cancer doctors and the kids were back in their seasonal routines. Truly the calm before the storm as the lingering trepidation remained, how much do I allow my expander to be filled. My first visit back to the office was simply to check to make sure I was healing correctly. The surgeon said I was doing great but was still a bit tight from the initial boost.

The following week Mike and I returned to the office for my first official expansion. I sat in a dental style of chair while the surgeon gathered two bottles of sterile saline and a needle the length of my foot. (I don't have small feet) It had a plastic casing on it that looked rather phallic. Mike couldn't resist the temptation and made an inquisitive joke wondering if in fact we were scheduled for the he/she package deal where we both got enhanced. Neither confirming nor denying Mike's inquiry my surgeon went about the task of filling me up.

Sitting in the chair I felt like I was in the laboratory with a mad scientist. However, rather than wearing a lab coat my doctor was wearing a standard looking suit and tie. To locate the place of insertion on the expander he had a little compass looking tool that had a metal detector on the end. As he waved it over my nicely healed incision the pointer fluctuated, much like my stud finder does when I am attempting to locate an appropriate place to hang a picture. Once found, he marked it with a pen then proceeded to inject me with not one foot long syringe but two of saline. I commented that I was going through puberty in a matter of five minutes, something that I had thought of often during this process. The surgeon conferred, "You're evolving from a fifth grader to a senior in high school."

The appointment lasted only a few minutes and although I had my extra-strength Tylenol handy, ready for consumption, I experienced no pain at all. The sensation was similar to what I felt when I was determined to get fit and lay on my back with a small weight on my chest doing sit-ups. It didn't hurt at all; it was just a little heavy. I was pleasantly surprised since, having been determined not to let my medical issues get in the way of our lives, our next stop was to pick up the kids and take them to the county fair. I still opted to pass on the rides, since I feared sloshing to and fro, but I enjoyed the family outing and celebration that life was good.

While Mike and the kids went on roller coasters and flying saucers my eyes often wandered. I found myself awkwardly caught up in my newfound hobby of noticing breasts. I evaluated which ones I found to be too big and which ones were just right, much like Goldilocks in the story of the *Three Bears*. Now, rather than physiologically developing into a young woman, I felt as though I had evolved into an adolescent boy. Everywhere I looked I saw breasts. I wondered what I looked like, what I would end up looking like and if other people would look at me and evaluate the size of my chest along with a judgment. I wondered if any of the gals that appeared to have enhanced breast came to the decision via a result of breast cancer or some other reason. Fortunately the fair offered many forms of entertainment so my observations remained a pastime rather than an obsession. We roamed from carnival games, to 3-D shows and through animal barns. It was a wonderful conclusion to a day that had started out a bit ambiguous. I was still the same woman, a mom who shared a wonderful time at the fair with her husband and kids. I wallowed joyfully in the normalcy and quietly applauded that my transformation remained a physical thing and not a mental one.

One week on and two weeks off seemed to be my medical schedule. During my reprieve, or more accurately my stretching time, I learned that I had some manipulative characteristics. Though the conversation of size had come up on more than one occasion between Michael and me, one evening I intentionally switched from my comfortable athletic style bra to a more traditional, form fitting one. It had a bit of an awkward fit, since my expander provided a crescent shaped lump rather than a traditional oval one, but none the less I could wear the bra and it did its job. I appeared more voluptuous than my daily look and my new side was bigger than my original. I felt my breasts screamed loud and clear from under my form fitting, scooped neck t-shirt. I guess I had anticipated a bit of an 'admission of defeat' from Mike. An, "Ah ha! You are bigger and better and we should stop while we are ahead," type of commentary. Instead, when I unleashed the inquisition (or was it an accusation?), "See, it would be silly to continue to grow" it was more of a deer in headlights. He didn't know which way to run for safety. I immediately knew he did not see things the same way as I did despite his loving reassurance that whatever I was comfortable with was what I should do.

He was smart enough to know that when I asked him for his opinion I wasn't really asking for *his* opinion. I was actually trying to manipulate him into conferring that what I thought was the sole truth. It was a no win situation for Mike so a, "Yes dear" was about the only peace keeping answer he could choke out.

With Mike away on travel for my next "fill" appointment I was on my own to determine the extent that I wanted to expand, and in my mind, please Mike. Though this fixation on breasts was really a miniscule issue it had a lifelong impact. The decision weighed heavily on my mind.

When Mike and I talked on the phone, hundreds of miles apart, it was as if there was a huge pink elephant in the room. After giving him the low down on each of the kids, and life on the home front, the conversation often circled back to my upcoming appointment. Of course, the discussion always began with him assuring me that size really didn't matter and that my comfort was most important. But then it circled back around to, "I think you would be happier being just a little bit bigger." What I interpreted that to mean was proportionally, either I was in denial and had a HUGE behind or disproportion is acceptable as long as it was in the right place. Either way it continued to be a no win exchange of words between the two of us. It was like I secretly wanted to stay a smaller size just to prove he didn't mean what he said about doing what I wanted and yet, I knew in the end all it would do was prove to me that he really did mean what he said. I knew that when it was all said and done he really didn't care about the size. It was like our daughter asking for a $200 pair of jeans. She wasn't going to be devastated by not getting them but in her mind it would be damn cool if she could. I was the one struggling with the whole concept of size, not him, and quite frankly I was tiring rather quickly from the psychological drama I had been creating.

The morning of my appointment I had decided to wear my bra and a camisole along with my highly casual taupe cargo pants. Rather than sticking to tradition and wearing my sports bra, I wanted the doctor to see what he was working with. I didn't want to falsify a flat chest, when in fact I was much more enhanced than when we started, and I didn't want to misrepresent myself as a high fashion, eager to entice 40 something either. Of course, it was all for nothing because I am always changed into the medical cape when he sees me, but somehow it made me feel better.

Mike called after I got Marcus off to school. He wanted to reiterate his support, and as much as I believed it was his intention he continued to tread in the benevolent space of support versus desire. I felt a little distant as I just wanted to dry my hair, put on a little mascara and carry on with my voyage. I knew he meant well but I could also read the message between the lines - *bigger is better,* whether real or imagined, and all I wanted to do was get off the phone and tackle the appointment, business as usual.

Arriving at the doctor's office I had no idle time in the waiting room. I was whisked away into the exam room happily avoiding my rather vain image of the curiosity of others. I envisioned people in the sitting area thinking, "In this economy is she really so selfish as to be spending money on breast enhancements?" As if they really cared about who I was or what I was doing. They had their own lives to ponder. I asked myself if my concern was just another reflection of my own judgmental character?

In the examination room I noticed a text from Mike. It read, "I love you just the way you are." I texted him back telling him "I know" and was in the middle of typing an additional text telling him I loved him just the way he was too when my phone rang. It was Mike calling to tell me that he was going to text me back something 'funny' about bigger is better but decided to call instead. He wanted to make sure that I knew he was kidding about the pending joke. This reminded me of the saying, "For everything there is a time. A time to dance, a time to sing, a time….." Well, this was no time for comedy and as much as it ate him up inside to not be with me for the appointment, it was apparent he was unaware of my genuine struggles. I had already had to redo my mascara twice because the morning tears had washed it away and no amount of joking was going to put my mind at ease.

The situation reminded me of a time just weeks earlier where Mike had been very hurt by something I had said when he was on our trampoline with Marcus. I had made a comment about him appearing to be rather inflexible when jumping. My intention was not to cast judgment on him; rather I was offering insight to the benefits of limbering up. Obviously I had not intended to cause offense to him, which he knew, but it was the fact that I didn't realize what he was going through that caused him the pain. It was a huge, courageous endeavor for him to go on the trampoline since one of the biggest difficulties from his MS is balance issues. Mike was rising to the occasion of jumping on the trampoline, despite all of his angst, since I was out of commission for a while and I had ruined the moment with a thoughtless comment. I felt awful as soon as the words came out of my mouth and for days I was appalled at my insensitivity. Now, with the tables turned and the reality of what is obvious to one person is not so obvious to the other, I was reliving that scenario. Michael was offering me insight to the benefits of having an enhanced chest and yet despite his wise observations it just wasn't that easy for me.

Marcus had been quite perceptive months earlier when he claimed that Mike and I would be able to better understand where each of us was coming from with our own aliments. Never had it been as apparent as just then.

I cut my conversation short with Mike as I reassured him that I would call him when I was done. With pen in hand I began to write all of my discombobulated feelings in my journal. Though never truly a safe thing to do, traveling with ones inner most thoughts sprawled across the lines of a notebook, I had anticipated a free moment or two to ejaculate my mixed up emotions. After feverishly writing a paragraph or two the surgeon entered the exam room. He greeted me by name and asked how things were going. After a quick evaluation of the surgical site he asked how I was feeling on size. With tears trickling down my cheeks I asked, "If you inject more today, and I determine that it is too big, can I decrease in size before it becomes permanent?" Confirming that the size could still be adjusted I complacently took my spot in the chair as he gathered the necessary paraphernalia to complete the enlargement.

With his back towards me, he filled the syringe. My attempts to wipe away the tears that continuously trickled from my eyes was unsuccessful. He handed me a tissue and, without missing a beat inserted the needle into the previously identified spot. He proceeded to infuse the fluid content into my expander. Feeling a bit awkward, wearing my emotions on my sleeve, I felt compelled to at least briefly explain the reason for my tears. (Not that my plastic surgeon would have internalized my emotional distress, but I couldn't help but think how I would feel if I had to walk into a room to treat someone who was crying, with-out any explanation.) So once I had been fully injected I simply asked if it was normal for a mastectomy patient to experience such mixed up emotions about reconstruction. His response revealed why he had not become overwhelmed by my sensitivity. He explained to me that it was very common for patients such as me to be a little anxious about the final destination. He compared it to a soon to be home owner that appears on a vacant plot of land with the illusion and vision of what the house will look like after construction. Although the image can be thought of, it can't actually be realized until the house is completed. The same could be said for the woman who is having a breast recreated. I couldn't help but wonder what his response would have been if I had asked about the homeowner who showed up to the piece of land which had a spectacular waterfront view and deemed she had no desire to build a mansion or even a two story home, but in fact was pitching her tent to be lived in for all eternity. Not that my plot of land was waterfront quality but I was satisfied living in modesty.

I shared with the doctor that I did not want to have to avoid wearing tank tops, for fear of being flamboyant, and declared that I had no desire to compete for the attention that my beautiful teenage daughter got. At which point he clarified, "Do or don't want to compete?" "DON'T!" I adamantly made clear. He then drew an appointment ending conclusion for me, "We are not changing who you are." And then he suggested, candidly, that I just needed to readjust my thinking to accept that truth. He even joked that maybe I would become a plastic surgery junky. A light hearted end to the deeply rooted conversation and quite frankly, the same conclusion Mike had been trying to draw for me all along.

WINK

Chapter Twenty-four

Now I felt somewhat like a human teeter-totter going from breasts which were as symmetrical as the human body was capable of making, to having one breast, then having a reconstructed mound that continued to creep beyond the limits of my natural one. For a Libra, (which I am one), the imbalance was becoming disconcerting. Standing in the bathroom evaluating my figure I decided it was time to reacquaint myself with my swimform, the prosthetic I had used prior to the expander surgery, only this time it was to enhance my untarnished side. As I inserted it into my bra I became the balanced scale I aspired to be.

Days continued to pass and I began feeling as though I had a grapefruit attached to my chest. I had fewer comfortable sleeping positions, since the ripening of my fruit, and my sports bras had even begun to feel uncomfortable. The perpetual evaluation of breast size clogged my mind and I wondered why I just couldn't jump on board to the whole idea of being grateful for the perk of implants after having to have a mastectomy. Then it came to me... I don't find big breasts attractive. It was a revelation! It wasn't that I didn't want to look as fabulous as I could; I just didn't lump, for lack of a better word, voluptuous breast into characteristics of beauty. In all the years of comparing myself to other women or evaluating beauty, breasts were not eye catching to me.

I think it is human nature to notice other people, whether they are the same gender or the opposite and form an automatic visual response. Isn't that what the racks full of magazines perpetuate? In thinking to myself what I have always found attractive, I realized it has consistently been a more average build with toned muscles in both men and women. So, although I had been hanging on to the belief that my disappointment and ungratefulness was from the idea of losing the saggy breasts that I had worked so hard to obtain in reality it was the idea that the bigger breasts weren't going to help make me more attractive and quite frankly, in my opinion, they were going to do quite the opposite. I figured out that I would be more appreciative of all the medical co-pays and deductibles if they were being spent on a kick ass personal trainer rather than a plastic surgeon, nothing personal to him, and I would be happier with the end result. This was quite a discovery for me; and since it is said, "The truth can set you free" I was hoping for some reprieve from my current bodily disappointment.

Realizing I wasn't a masochist and still stuck in the dysfunctional belief systems from Louise Hay's book, I felt a sense of relief. I had in fact evolved through this experience and was beginning to believe the mantras. Without a full conscious awareness I had accepted the *cancer*'s new thought pattern, "I lovingly forgive and release all of the past. I choose to fill my world with joy. I love and approve of myself." I had begun to release the false idea that I had to hang onto the saggy, or deflated 41, now 42, year old breasts. I could love and approve of myself without the shame I had orchestrated in connection to a phony me with fake breasts. It was an extremely freeing experience and surely a step towards a healthy happy body.

It was somewhat ironic that after my revelation I sat down to watch an episode of Desperate Housewives and one of the main story lines focused on the obsession with big breasts. Lynette Scavo, one of the 'Desperate Housewives' had become unexpectedly pregnant and as a result had begun to look rather busty. Though a common side effect of pregnancy, she had allowed the people she worked with to believe she had had implants because she was not ready to divulge the truth about her 'true twins' that were on the way. Throughout the entire episode men had eye contact with her breasts rather than her eyes. Men and women both were mesmerized by her appearance as she walked by revealing her voluptuous breasts. The show went on to reveal both her disappointment with mankind and her mystification with their obsession of breasts. Of course, her husband saved the day when he conveyed why he loved her with or without the big breasts.

The writers of the show did a wonderful job capturing the dilemma women face when they feel they don't measure up as well as when they measure up by false pretenses. However, they also revealed how initial disappointment can be just as easily swapped for complacency and true contentment.

True contentment was exactly what I had slid into over the past few months. Sure, I had appointments here and there and the nuisance of reconstruction but health wise I had been cured of cancer and my revelations had begun to slip.

Though I was still drinking green tea each day, my coffee intake had managed to surpass the allotted one to two cups per day mark. I had let my healthy eating and exercising ways also diminish and could feel the effects. No longer facing the fear of disease I was surprised at how quickly I had abandoned the higher level of thinking. Why was it so easy to just coast along rather than be actively engaged?

During this time of complacency my dad ended up in the hospital with pneumonia and what the doctors thought to be complications from the growth of his cancer. They informed us that they were a bit concerned, considering he had been given numerous varieties of chemo therapy and his body no longer seemed to be responding. I had a compassionate but truthful talk with my dad and advised him that he needed to take care of things that meant the most to him.

After nearly three years of fighting a terminal disease my dad had shared little with me about himself, his wishes in this life, his thoughts of the world beyond, and never had he once conveyed to me what his life had meant to him. I knew little of his childhood, the things in life that he was the most proud of or the sorriest for. He hadn't shared with me any hopes of a legacy which he wanted to leave behind. Since he never had a son the family name would no longer be carried on and it was a little sad that, even now, I didn't know what generations to come would find if they ever delved into the family crest.

These thoughts were resonating within me. How had I been on the verge of a horrendous encounter, staring fear straight in the eyes, sure that I would elevate myself as a human being as I conquered the disease and then so quickly deserted the idea? How had I vowed to no longer take my husband, my family, or my life for granted and then, just a few months later, have awoken from the nightmare as if it had all been pretend? Just as easily as the dream faded, so had my valiant ideas of resurrection; and without warning I had returned to my gluttonous ways.

WINK

Chapter Twenty-five

Perhaps gluttony was what was necessary for me to accept the next step in my journey as I ventured back to the plastic surgeon's office to have my non-mastectomy side worked on; to better match the manmade breast that I would be left with post-mastectomy. Since I had become so indifferent to the residual effects of my breast cancer it was getting easier to just go with the flow rather than taking it all so seriously. Obviously I had had an easier ride compared to most that had been diagnosed with cancer. I was spared chemotherapy and radiation along with all of their devastating side effects. I felt a sense of guilt even being lumped into the category of 'survivor' because to me, the title represented such bravery.

The night before surgery even the universe seemed to confirm the blasé attitude I had earned for my inconsequential bout with cancer. We had gotten together for a large, extended family dinner at a nearby Chinese restaurant. At the completion of the meal everyone chose their fortune cookie. Mine didn't have a fortune in it but Mike's couldn't have been any more appropriate. It read: 'your love life is going to soon be enhanced'. Even our daughter Karli noticed the irony in the words. This superstitious piece of paper seemed to, rather eloquently, sum up the experience.

This laid a clear pathway to my appointment. After following the routine of changing into my gown and folding my clothes into my surgical bin, Mike asked me if I wanted him to take a picture of my breast as a memento. I had no desire to have a bare-breasted shot on his iPhone; but just as I turned down his proposition I was quickly called in to the black and white room with the plastic surgeon. Of course, when I returned Mike couldn't help but joke about the injustice.

The surgeon then proceeded to draw somewhat of a circle around my existing breast. As he did he commented about how one lady almost fainted in fear that he was marking the cutting line, which of course would have left a scar in its place. He assured me that my scar wouldn't even come close in size. Then, I don't quite remember how, the conversation turned and the surgeon guaranteed that I wouldn't be cheated in size. I declared to him that it was the opposite that concerned me and he promised I wouldn't tip over when he was done either.

Having become a completed canvas I again put on the gown; the anesthesiologist came in to ask me some questions about when I last ate. As she left, the nurse appeared inquiring about additional routine topics, advised Mike and me that it was time for our 'goodbyes', led me to the restroom and finally into the operating room. This was a well oiled machine that, sad to say, I was becoming all too familiar with how it ran.

I climbed onto the operating table, was covered with my favorite warm air-flowing blanket, and was hooked up to all of the operating room gadgets. This time I was sedated and the surgeon applied a local anesthetic as opposed to being put under with the heavy drugs. It was a quick, easy surgery and I embraced the gradual sleepy feeling rather than the sharp pains that typically ran up my arm.

I awoke, fully clothed, sitting in a wheelchair, ready to head home. Having been put under a total of four times, with no memory of getting dressed with any of them, I thought it would be fun to video tape the whole process. I imagined it looking like a life-size game of dolls, slinging arms through sleeves and zipping up sweatshirts. It seemed like it would be pretty difficult to manage all that dead weight but somehow I had always been properly reassembled.

Again, I went home, was banished to bed to fall in and out of sleep. Thankfully sleepiness was the only side effect from the medication but the repeated wasted days began to annoy me. I was obedient the day after surgery and pretty much laid low. Once I finished reading my romance novel, I no longer had anything enticing me to relax. With the numerous surgeries and recoveries even my family seemed indifferent with the mundane routine. No longer worried that I would somehow have a mishap, my caretaking consisted of barks to stay in bed. I think this was more because I had not graciously accepted the previous pampering, always reassuring everyone of my self-sufficiency; though, strangely enough, I missed it now that I didn't have it. The repetitiveness of the latest surgery was just another reminder of how, despite my good intentions of evolving enlightened from this potentially life threatening experience, the only thing that had really changed was my body and even that had become boring.

With Thanksgiving holidays just around the corner the alteration in my breast, with the new implant, simply reminded me of a stuffed belly after a big meal. The difference wasn't astounding just fuller and obviously, unlike after overeating, I couldn't sleep this one off. It was here to stay. Though Mike thought it looked nice I was indifferent to it.

With the limitations of what I could do and wear I vowed that, once and for all, I would stop taking life for granted. I would stop procrastinating about exercise, healthy eating, spiritual growth, walks with the dog and most importantly – spending quality time with family and friends. Though I had grown critical of my father's lack of gratitude for second chances, I realized that I had misdirected my frustration; I was the one to be appalled with. How many second chances did I need before I committed myself to change?

WINK

Chapter Twenty-six

Since I was still on the "take it easy" prescription I decided what better time to re-instigate change with Karli, a teenager in the midst of bidding for her independence. Though I saw independence as her ability to become self-sufficient she saw it more as the ability to self-rule. Though synonyms, these words have very different meanings. I envisioned a clean room, minimal time being squandered watching television and perusing the computer and no more petty fights with Marcus; she visualized not being told what and when to do anything. Despite my inconsistencies of evolution I had continued to reflect on my mothering style, thanks to Louise Hay, and decided that Karli and I were still in search of a middle ground between my over-mothering and her idle behavior.

I had made great strides in minimizing my controlling ways in at least one aspect of her life; with her driving. When she first got her permit I often overreacted with visions of my life flashing before my eyes. Trying to have power over the situation I continuously barked commands and gave ultimatums. Despite my amped up domination Karli managed to stay calm and in charge behind the wheel. After my surgeries, when life really did flash before my eyes, I realized control was just a fallacy. No longer able to orchestrate everything into my nice and tidy plan I took a deep breath and began enjoying the ride. Karli continued to prove herself to be a fabulous driver time and time again. We still have our occasional explosion in the car but usually it is a pretty smooth drive. The only thing that has changed, aside from a bit more experience on Karli's part, is my ability to relinquish control. It hasn't been so easy in other parts of her life.

One of the painstaking issues I have with Karli is the amount of television she watches. Considering I would find great joy in eliminating our cable bill altogether I may be a bit biased in assessing what is too much, but none the less it eats at me. Most of the shows she watches are reality shows ranging from hairstyle competitions to "Real Housewives". Though I believe most of them contain as much reality as the Flintstones, they do occasionally portray real life experiences. On one particular show the cameras shadowed a gal going to get breast augmentations. This instigated curiosity in Karli and curiosity can often lead to learning. I decided to invite Karli to join me for my post implant surgery since she was out of school and Mike was out of town. Throughout the various stages of my cancer saga she had occasionally asked to see the progress. She never appeared to be too surprised by what she saw and actually, rather indifferent.

Though initially I thought she would remain in the waiting area during my exam, I realized that a learning opportunity such as this may not come again. I admitted to her that I was a bit uncomfortable with the whole idea of her sitting there while my male doctor lifted and looked at my breast's progress but she suggested, "It can't be as bad for me as it is for Dad." Since Karli is much more at ease with the human body than I am, and she did have a point about Mike's discomfort. I decided to let her join me. As we were escorted down the hall and through the open door the typical examination room had magically changed into a science lab. I only had a moment to familiarize Karli with the room before my doctor joined us. Still fumbling with the gown I made introductions and explained that had I brought Karli along so she could decide if she ever wanted to become a plastic surgeon. My doctor asked if she was really interested in the field. I admitted that she was more interested in the procedures themselves than performing them so I was hoping to reveal the painstaking reality of plastic surgery and to cure her from ever wanting to have anything done. He suggested that there was no need in detouring her at such an early age, implying future patients needed to come from somewhere.

After his usual dry humored bantering he removed my stitches told Karli that I would be a hottie by spring, bragging more about the quality of his work than complimenting me personally. Karli was quick minded, just like Mike, and rather than dwell on the surgeon's comments she simply replied, "Then I guess I am going to have to go to the guys' houses rather than having them over to mine." The only thing entertaining about the whole conversation was Karli's quick wit, as the topic gave me the heebie-jeebies.

Next, I was taken off guard when my doctor decided that a small injection was in order for my expander. I was under the impression that I was done with my growth spurt. It turned out to be a much more informative visit for Karli than I had expected. The surgeon gathered a saline bottle, a long syringe and an iodine swab. He performed the procedure with graceful precision, stuck a small round band-aid on the insertion site and advised me that I was done for the day. Karli didn't seem too distressed by the appointment; actually she seemed rather enamored by the assortment of plastic surgery procedures that various people in the clinic had had. Though unrecognizable to me I found her explanations fascinating. Even though I had been visiting the plastic surgeon's office for over five months I never had any idea of the scope of work that was done behind closed doors.

WINK

Chapter Twenty-seven

Tick tock, tick tock. I counted the days, the hours, the minutes until I could get back to full throttle. The inactive lifestyle had run its course and I no longer felt compliant. My expander would be coming out in one and a half months and I felt like a young child anxiously awaiting Santa Claus just after Halloween when all the toy commercials begin; and about as patient.

With my attention always seeming to circle around to my breasts, I began to realize that despite the fact that my check-up appointment had gone well, with everything looking good on the implant side, a peculiar sensation had failed to dissipate even after nearly three weeks. Originally I thought it was the local anesthetic taking a while to wear off. Considering my mastectomy side was still basically numb to the bone after five plus months I didn't think much of a couple of weeks. The feeling was like the prickly sense that I get when my foot falls asleep. It wasn't painful but the pins and needle feeling was unpleasant when anything rubbed on it. Not really the circumstance a husband wants to hear exists after his wife acquires a fresh new ta-ta.

With no interest in wanting Mike to manhandle the new goods I decided it was time to check in with the doctor's office. I called and asked to speak to the nurse. After giving the details of my condition to the receptionist she conveyed her understanding of the situation and assured me that the feeling was normal. She explained that my nerves were repairing themselves from surgery and they were hypersensitive. She said that for some people just the movements of clothing on their chest made them want to crawl out of their skin. Counting my blessings I thanked her for the information and decided I didn't need any more reassurance of the normalcy of my prickly feelings from the higher ups. Though she had said it could take a few months I was confident the wee bee gee bee feelings would pass much quicker for me.

Sure enough as soon as I got wind of the normalcy of my sensation I relaxed a bit and let my guard down. The uncomfortable feelings began to dissipate and I was beginning to feel close to normal. Well, as normal as one person could feel with a solid lump still protruding from one side. It was still another month with my expander but the newly 'enhanced' side was becoming more acceptable. Still, when Mike asked how I liked it my response was not much more exciting than someone being asked if they liked squid or liverwurst better. The size and shapes of breast were still uninteresting to me especially now that my volume had somewhat been determined. My attitude had not miraculously changed. The whole 'boob job' was still just a 'matter of fact' thing.

One thing that did change was my outlook as to what was important. One cannot help but evaluate life when an illness confronts you. As I asked myself what I would regret if I were to have died from all of this, aside from missing out on the lives of my family, the only thing that rang true was my lack of worldly travel. Pretty fortunate for a person to merely regret that, but none-the-less it was the one disappointment that life offered me. Strangely enough, when I started this whole journey I was reading about geographical adventure. Who would have known back then that it was the only hunger I would continue to experience.

Although I wasn't at a time in my life where I felt I could just pick up and roam the global grounds, our daughter had longed to attend a high school overseas. The program's session lasted for two month. Until now I had never given it any serious consideration, after all she was only 15 years old, but with all the events of the past year I said to Mike, "There's no time like the present".

So, without letting the grass grow under our feet we filled out the paperwork, got her passport renewed and sent her on her merry way. I felt proud that we were giving Karli the gift of travel so that she would never have the same regret as I.

Strangely enough, it didn't occur to me until she was there, experiencing amazing things first hand, that perhaps I was still caught in the reoccurring idea of not putting my needs first. Sure, these thoughts only came to me after I was a bit perturbed having learned she pierced her nose and double pierced her ear leaving a bar running through it, all of which she assured me sounded worse than it looked. I wondered how I had determined it wasn't a good time for me to travel but I easily justified it for our daughter. After regaining my sound mind, realizing that holes in the head are the least of our parenting worries, and remembering the benefits we were providing her by allowing her to be venturing out among the broader human race, I was grateful that Karli had helped me to see it was time to start planning my own worldly travels. The European cruise I had been dreaming of needed to be shifted towards the top of the 'to do' list. There **is** no time like the present. And just like that I moved from my hobby of wandering eyes to planning our next family vacation overseas.

WINK

Chapter Twenty-eight

With two days until surgery, when they planned to take out my expander- the crescent shaped device that had become hard and felt like it protruded from the area under my arm, I was on my nesting mission. It was a race to make it through my list of chores. Vacuum, laundry, wash the dog, shopping, school projects, the quick pace was energizing as was the idea that I would soon be able to enjoy a comfortable night sleep no matter what position I laid in.

Having completed my mundane tasks, the surgery day arrived much different than the others. Mike was away on a business trip, Karli was away on her foreign journey and Marcus was off to school. My mom was appointed my valiant chauffer and now destined to get the behind the scenes look whether she wanted to or not. The morning started off a bit tumultuous with Karli continuing to exercise her independence over the phone. I was amazed that such emotional discord could take place with her so many miles away but we eventually resolved the conflict allowing me to return to my harmonious state of chi.

The doctor's office called and said they were ahead of schedule and asked if I could come in an hour early. It was ironic, considering the numerous surgical delays we had experienced, that Mike wasn't here for the early appointment. I slipped into my 'going in for surgery' outfit that consisted of pull on sweatpants, a t-shirt, a zip-up sweatshirt and slip on shoes. They were all items easy to get on and off. We turned off the lights, locked the door behind us and were on our way. Providing driving directions I advised my mom to turn right here, turn left there and with-in minutes we had arrived.

Once out of the elevator I commented to mom, as I did to each of my newcomers, how the clinic itself was rather busy and cluttered but advised her to notice the difference as we came upon the plastic surgeons' office. Rich wood planks lined the wall with each of the surgeons' names scrolled in crisp, black letters. It was always comical to me entering through the frosted glass door into the waiting room. It felt as though I had walked through the wardrobe in the children's story *The Lion, The Witch and the Wardrobe* as the change was nearly as dramatic. This time the distinction was even more obvious as the office had just been freshly painted in a warm caramel color that complimented the comfortable earth toned chairs provided to recline in. The feeling in the office, as opposed to the clinic, was luxurious. I suppose this was intentional since plastic surgery was often a bit indulgent.

Shortly after I checked in at the front desk mom and I were escorted into the examination room. After talking with the nurse and the anesthesiologist we had received all of the post operation details and instructions and I had signed my life away on various wavers. Left to change into the patient gown we were told the doctor would be in momentarily. Sure enough he came in to the room in true form, self-assured and business as usual, and whisked me away for my standard bare-breasted shot. I had been dreading this picture taking session. The holidays had just passed and I had the joy of starting my period prior to surgery this time both of which made me a bit plumper than before. Thankfully, my plastic surgeon didn't make any snide comments as I disrobed for the camera. With-out time to doddle I barely got my gown on to cross the hall and return to the examination room for him to draw out his surgical plan. Looking around the newly painted room he asked, more to himself than to my mom and me, "Where's my butt holder?" referring to his rolling doctor stool. I don't think he intended to be humorous but the reference was rather amusing. He excused himself to find it and upon his return I introduced him to my mom. With-out skipping a beat he smoothly replied, "Your sister?" and continued to draw the lines that would define the volume of my new breast. We confirmed that the aim was to use a saline implant, unless in surgery he deemed it was not a viable option. I always opted for low maintenance and saline was certainly more preferable than silicone under those criteria.

Knowing my doctor, and the pride he had in his reputation, I was sure that he would provide me with a look of perfection at the mastectomy site. I felt secure with the reality that my future figure was in his hands; though, if you had asked me a year ago I would never have imagined proclaiming delight with my breasts being in the hands of another man.

All marked up and ready for action my mom and I said our goodbyes. She returned to the waiting room and I ventured on to the surgical suite, with one short stop at the restroom. Patients are not allowed to have any apparatuses on or in their body so with-out contacts and only a pad for protection I prayed that my bodily functions would slow when they put me under for surgery. Once in the surgical room I climbed aboard the table, got hooked up to the various machines and chatted with the staff about the female anatomy. There was no consensus as to whether menopause and hot flashes were better or worse than pre-menopause and all the womanly issues one faces. I guess it didn't really matter though because both come at various stages in life, ready or not.

With the familiar paper blanket covering me, with warm air flowing through, I received the warning that I would be getting sleepy. The whole phenomenon of going under is a little peculiar. One minute I am completely awake and talking then the next minute I feel a little dizzy, decide to close my eyes and then, as if no time has passed at all I am awake. This time I woke up even sooner, just as the nurse was putting on my t-shirt. I felt so proud to be able to help re-dress rather than being the limp, lifeless ragdoll I imagined myself having been all the other times. The nurse informed me that everything went well. She handed me a small card and directed me to keep it in a safe place as it contained information regarding the saline implant they had just put embedded in me. As soon as the wheelchair arrived I was guided down the hall to greet my mom.

I heard the surprise in my mom's voice when the nurse called out to her that I was done. "Already?" she asked. Sure enough the surgery had taken less than an hour and a half, pretty amazing since they opened me up, took out the expander, put in the implant, compared symmetry, and then closed me back up. We were on our way home in no time and I called Mike to tell him it was over. Then Karli called, 12:30am her time, to make sure everything went okay. This made all of our previous arguments seem trivial. The confirmation I needed to remind me that she clearly had a warm loving heart and whose feelings extended beyond her egocentric teenage boundaries. Whether it was the residual anesthetic lingering in my system or true emotional delight I was completely content. My spirits were high and I felt fortunate that this chapter in my life was nearing its end.

Once home I obediently climbed in bed and dozed on and off throughout the rest of the day. When Marcus got home he was happy to join me for a low key evening of watching television, something I rarely do. I fell in and out of sleep, according to the rhythm of the phone ringing. The well wishes were a familiar tune that warmed my heart. I wished that everyone could be so lucky as to have such an abundance of love and care. I drifted off to sleep counting down the hours until I could be in full function again.

Recovery from the surgery was simple, although when I was ready to take my shower I wondered to myself why on earth I had worn my favorite gray v-neck t-shirt to surgery. Though made of soft, woven cotton which feels comfortable on my skin the ribbing on the neckline provided constraints that made it difficult to get out of. When I originally helped get it back on after surgery I was a bit more pliable from the medication. For each of my other surgeries I was simply redressed in my sweatshirt, forgoing anything underneath, which at this point in time made a lot more sense. I decided that the help I provided in maneuvering my arm through the small opening hadn't been such a great thing after all and I was a bit perplexed how to get it off.

I turned off the shower, which had already been running long enough that the hot water from the downstairs water heater had managed to flow through the maze of copper pipes and steam had begun to form on the bathroom mirror inhibiting my ability to observe myself attempting to contort out of the shirt. Fortunately, just days earlier I had discovered an application on my son's IPod touch called "Unblock Me" and had solved more than my share of puzzles. Strangely enough it is a game that requires one to move blocks vertically and horizontally in order to release one red block through a small opening. The challenge was always so gratifying. Who knew it had come to me merely as a post surgical training program? With my freshly sharpened skills I lifted one side of the shirt then the other and decided I needed to get my non-surgery side arm out of the shirt first in order to be able to lift the shirt over my head and allow the other arm the freedom to slide out. Just as the blocks moved in very specific directions my body was only willing to be pushed and pulled in particular ways. Finally I "unblocked" my arm and was free from my beloved t-shirt.

Looking into the de-fogged mirror I was happy to see a more natural form taking shape on my chest. For the most part it looked pretty darn good. I did notice that it appeared to be a bit swollen and a little pink around the incision sight. Though I would usually turn to Mike for reassurance that everything looked as it should, with him out of town I resorted to using a hand held mirror to get a better view from a variety of angles. Still unsure of the normalcy I went to my mom to ask her opinion. Being a good sport she analyzed my breast as I verbally went down the post-surgical check list determining that it wasn't overly hot or painful and I didn't have a fever. So when I proclaimed, "I'm sure it's fine," she concurred.

I returned to take my shower, which felt soothing, but I couldn't keep from wondering if everything really was okay. Rather than allowing myself to become a hypochondriac I got dressed and went about my leisurely day. I continued to take extra-strength Tylenol as directed but it was more a formality than a necessity. There was no pain to speak of, and very little discomfort, but I felt the need to perpetually check on the area in question which had appeared to be widening. I made no mention of my concerns to Mike when he called since there was nothing he could do and I didn't want to worry him. I knew everything was fine and it was just my mind getting the best of me.

When asked how things were I continued to respond that things were going well.

As the evening rolled around my mom encouraged me to call the doctor just for peace of mind. Of course, by the time I decided to call, the office was closed but the operator offered to page the surgeon. Remembering my last "on call" interaction with my doctor, where my side jowls were nothing to speak of, I knew this situation was just the same so I opted not to have him paged. I decided I was fine since I still lacked a fever or excruciating pain.

Despite having slept well I had become a little obsessive about the discoloration. No longer could I tell if the area was growing and quite frankly, having just had an implant put in I wasn't a good judge as to whether or not the area was swollen or not. I called the office and since it was Friday, with the weekend lurking, they wanted to have a look at it.

Feeling ridiculous for not having been able to comfort myself, and for not accepting the reassurance from my mom, I drove into the city for my doctor to have a peak. The whole encounter took minutes. My doctor looked at it, drew along the perimeters with a permanent marker and told me if it grew beyond the boarder that I should take a picture, email it to him and call him so we could talk about it. His expert opinion suggested that it was just bruising from the surgery. Go figure that not all bruises are black and blue! He informed me that if I was ultra worried he could prescribe an antibiotic just for peace of mind. In order to prevent being perceived as a neurotic patient, and considering I am not a fan of taking unnecessary drugs, I assured him that I had no need for frivolous antibiotics and would just watch it. Leaving, I felt proud that I had been responsible enough to obtain the professional reassurance I knew Mike would have wanted me to get. By the time I got home the pink discoloration had miraculously began to subside. There was really nothing to even tell Mike about. I had been silly to have even worried.

Everything had settled down and aside from not doing anything strenuous, and being a little bored, all was good. That was until we got home from the airport with Mike. After discussions about his trip, and my well-being, I mentioned that I had gone to the doctor the day before. I'm still not sure how things managed to spiral out of control, with my telling him I didn't like the tone he was using with me and vice-versa, but the evening was a disaster with barely a "goodnight" said to each other. Fortunately he had gotten home around 9:00pm so there wasn't a lot of time left for combat.

Not ones to go to bed mad, in-fact we have pillow cases stating, "Always Kiss Me Goodnight," I was able to pretend that we had each fallen asleep watching our latest Netflix movie rather than believing our avoidance had been intentional. The one problem was that when I awoke I had a lingering pit in my stomach caused by the residual effects of being misunderstood. Mike had been out of town on business, attending a trade show, during which time I had had surgery, the last thing we were supposed to be doing was arguing.

Pacifying my need for deep understanding and closure I sat at my computer typing a letter to Mike. While it was not unusual for him to receive my written words after an unsuccessful verbal exchange this time I chose not to send them to him. Instead, as I finished composing my thoughts, I conveyed that there was a parent learning session with our clergy during the time that Marcus was attending Sunday school. Typically I went solo, representing us both, mostly because I failed to give fair warning. I knew that after a long week at work Mike liked watching Sunday morning sports and unlike him, I did not attend religious school through the age of thirteen. For whatever reason, the late notice was disregarded as he quickly showered and joined me. Strangely enough the topic was about forgiveness. It covered many aspects of the act including a brainstorm session conjuring up a list of factors that needed to be in place for forgiveness to occur. It was interesting to learn that just as individuals often have their own stipulations for offering forgiveness so did various religions.

As informative as the entire lecture was, and as fascinating as it was to see how forgiveness was granted in biblical stories, I still didn't have a complete understanding of the topic. Though Mike and my situation was nowhere near the catastrophic wrong doings as in the bible, in my mind, I wondered what a person was supposed to do when she felt wronged but didn't feel as though she herself had wronged especially when, oddly enough, the other person felt the same way. After careful consideration I realized that marriage is often comprised of such events and perhaps fate had brought us together to hear the valuable information on forgiveness. We left the morning discussion laughing as we realized we both had the same lingering question regarding forgiveness.

At home I baited Mike by asking, "Do you want to talk about last night?" It took us a while to get to the bottom of the problem but on the surface he was hurt that I hadn't shared my post- surgery concerns with him. He was unhappy that I had repeatedly told him everything was fine regarding the surgery when in actuality it hadn't been. I defended myself by telling him that there was nothing he could have done, that I didn't want to worry him and quite frankly, (here's where the tide started to turn) I didn't want him second guessing me when he wasn't here to know what I was experiencing.

As in most quarrels, the longer the discussions go on, something eventually gets dislodged. Sometimes it is as if someone simply barfs all over the other with pent up trivial junk but at other times something very important is revealed. For us the later happened and it brought us both to tears. I realized that I was angry at Mike for not being there for me when I had surgery.

189

Wow, what a revelation! I pride myself on being self-sufficient, courageous, brave, strong... the warrior characteristics could go on and on and quite frankly it would honor me to think that others see me in a similar light. So imagine the surprise when I realized that those traits hinge on the one factor, that I have my yang (of yin and yang), Mike, by my side. I was very displeased. I was angry for not being as brave as I perceived myself to be and caught off guard by my neediness.

It sounds a bit harsh, after nearly 20 years of marriage having a revelation of needing someone, but I believe part of Mike and my success in marriage is that we are independent of each other. We are like peanut butter (my favorite food) and jelly; we go together but aren't so enmeshed that we can't stand on our own. Ironically, I now realize that what has also contributed to our ability to triumph over the years is that we have been there for each other intuitively. We have been rather fortunate in being so insightful of each other's needs, up until this point. But even now I was certain that this mishap was pointing me into a new, healthier form of existence. Unbeknownst to him, Mike was helping me find my voice.

WINK

Chapter Twenty-nine

Upon Mike's return it was obvious our ebb and flow had been off. Neither one of us had realized how much I had needed him. I needed him to be barking stupid comments at me like I should be in bed even when I was simply getting up to use the restroom because those are the loving words that reassure me that everything is going to be okay. I didn't have that and I missed it and I was mad at him for not having known better.

I was mad at him for not being around to look at my breasts and evaluate them even though every other time I had been a bit put off by him wanting to constantly see them. It took him not looking at them for me to realize what compassion he was showing when he was looking. I had been forced to visit my doctor because Mike wasn't there.

Needless to say after the 'need' monster was unleashed in a strange, peculiar way I felt closer to Mike and a bit healthier. Though I wish I would have realized my need ahead of time it was good to know I was moving toward a healthier place. I was recognizing that taking on a warrior stance in life and attempting to take care of everything single handedly was a mistake. Even if I believed I was successful at it, I could see that eventually I may very well become resentful. Perhaps I would end up feeling my efforts went unnoticed or that I was taken for granted. Then, one day something could happen where I needed someone, only I wouldn't realize it until it was too late because I was never brave enough to let someone know I needed them.

I can't help but resort again to Louise Hay's book *Heal Your Body*. I turn to the topic of female problems and read the probable cause as: Denial of the self. Rejecting femininity. Rejection of the feminine principle. This too has been a festering issue inside me. Not that I am an extreme woman's libber but I do believe that the sexes are created equal and though there may be a few things that men can do that women can't, they are certainly evened out by the things that women can do that men can't.

I have now discovered, firsthand, what can happen when pride is allowed to cloud the truth. Though I will continue to strive to be as self-sufficient as possible I will no longer be so disillusioned that I believe that it is valiant to go it alone. I am comforted by the awareness that I need Mike. I have discovered that the pain is not in needing someone; it's in needing them and realizing that they aren't there. I am learning that it is my responsibility to communicate my needs and how important it is that I teach our children how to do the same. As a breast cancer survivor it is my responsibility to continue to heal. In assisting me to do so, I embrace the new thought pattern suggested by Louise Hay for female problems and the mantra which is stated as: "I rejoice in my femaleness. I love being a woman. I love my body."

As I look into the mirror, topless, I observe that my body's restoration is quite natural. Still not being a "breast" person, the two lumps now just make me appear symmetrically plum, but the goal of putting me back together has been reached with great success. It's hard to remember what my chest looked like after my mastectomy. Although I recall that I wasn't horrified by the sight, and from time to time have missed the **idea** of a cheerful wink staring back at me from the mirror, I am very grateful that I went ahead with reconstruction. Except for the lack of a nipple, which I will receive in a month or so, my breast could pass as real and that means that my life is just about back to normal.

I transformed from a 41 year old with "deflated" breasts, to a lopsided mastectomy patient with a wink, to a peculiar looking cartoon character and now returning to a more natural state of being with two symmetrical, nothing too unusual looking, breasts. I am happy with the size, as they are not something I feel I will need to hide in oversized sweatshirts and yet they do not require the support of an underwire bra with back straps crossing this way and that. It is as the oncologist suggested many months back, that despite the downsides of being diagnosed with Ductal Carcinoma In-situ I have evolved with a somewhat improved physique. (If you ignore the extra holiday pounds which I am sure to work off once I receive the green light to resume exercise). Overall, I have basically concluded my journey with great success.

At first glance the changes that have taken place over these past few months have merely been reduced to physical alterations despite my intentions to find the deeper meaning in life, but when I stop and think about the time that has passed I have learned so much more. I do have a greater respect for life. I realize I can no longer take for granted my ability to do what I want when

I want. As Marcus so wisely stated upon learning the news, I have gained some insight to the frustration that Mike experiences daily by limitations put on his body. Because of this I aspire to be more understanding of the efforts he, and many people have to make in order to accomplish tasks that most of us find mundane. I am more aware of the love that surrounds us and the obligation I have, whether it is comfortable or not, to extend myself to others in need. It is becoming more clear to me that in order to heal I have to work on myself. I can't give to others in hopes of receiving myself and I can't seek noble causes to fight for in order to avoid confronting my own internal struggles. Most recently, I realized that it is important to let others know I need them and it is just as import to recognize it myself. For even though peanut butter is good on its own it usually tastes better with an accompaniment.

Life is a journey that takes us in many mysterious directions. I feel blessed that this experience has left me safe and a bit more sound.

My heart goes out to all who suffer whether it is from cancer, multiple sclerosis, the multitude of other diseases or tragedies or even daily disappointments. I hope that one day we can all be healed by the love and care that surrounds us and come together in unity with a cure for everyone.

Bon voyage!

Acknowledgements

I would like to thank my mom, my aunt Jeanine and my mother-in-law for reading numerous versions of my story and for believing in me.

I am grateful to my doctors for their expertise and for making the journey through breast cancer a blip in the road as opposed to a nightmare.

A very special thanks to Michael Townley for sharing her editing expertise with me and helping me get on the right track with word usage and phrasing.

I would like to thank Jane Rosenstein for being open to share her story and offer such courage. I hope everyone diagnosed with disease has a "Jane".

Finally, to my husband Michael (Mike) who believes all things are possible and inspires me to dream big and also to my children, I want to thank each of you for your love which makes every day so special.